Feeding the Sheep

# FEEDING THE SHEEP

## THE

# SHEEP

## BENJAMIN S. BAKER

BROADMAN PRESS
Nashville, Tennessee

Dewey Decimal Classification: 253
Subject Headings: MINISTERS // CHRISTIAN SOCIAL MINISTRIES
Library of Congress Catalog Number: 85-15139

Printed in the United States of America

**Library of Congress Cataloging in Publication Data**

Baker, Benjamin S. (Benjamin Stanley)
   Feeding the sheep.

   Sequel to: Shepherding the sheep.
   Bibliography: p.
   1. Service (Theology) 2. Church charities.
3. Pastoral theology. I. Title.
BT738.4.B34 1985        253        85-15139
ISBN 0-8054-2544-6

*This work is dedicated to the
least of these my brethren.*

# Contents

# Acknowledgments

Many persons have invested their information, insights, and illuminative thoughts in this writer. I have merely withdrawn on those priceless deposits.

I want to honor the benelovent labor of love expressed by the typing of this book by Mrs. Barbara Johnson and Mrs. Mildred Bailey, two faithful servants of the Main Street Baptist Church, Lexington, Kentucky.

The Lord providentially placing me in a Christian home which nourished and nurtured me in the ministry of compassion certainly has enhanced my own sensitivity to the needs of others.

And finally my love must be expressed to my wife Carol, who is "My Inn in the Wilderness," who constantly kept telling me, "You can do it; stick with it." For her encouragement and mothering of our four children Brian, Beth, Benne, and Bennice I am grateful.

BENJAMIN S. BAKER
LEXINGTON, KENTUCKY
April, 1985

# Preface

The intent of this book is to put into the hands of pastors, church staff persons, and all disciples of Jesus Christ who are conscious of and compassionate with their Lord's demand, "inasmuch as ye have done it unto one of the least of these, my brethren ye have done it unto me" (Matt. 25:40, KJV), a working manual that will help in the day-by-day practice of ministry.

Six models will be considered, all drawn from those our Lord refers to in Matthew 25:31-44. These are the hungry, the thirsty, the stranger, the naked, the sick, and the prisoner.

Each area of ministry will be considered first from the biblical perspective as to what our Lord has said in both the Old and New Testaments. Second, a ministry strategy will be developed for our contemporary settings. Third, guidelines for present and future ministries will be presented.

If this work can help in the feeding of God's sheep, then He, the Good Shepherd, will be glorified.

This book has been written for the disciple of Jesus Christ who has heard the personal, probing, penetrating question being asked by Jesus, "Do you love me?" and who has responded in the affirmative, "Yes, Lord." To this response Jesus has said, "Feed My sheep."

In Matthew 25:35-36, Jesus gives the specific areas in

which His sheep need feeding. This book addresses each one of those areas; that is, how to feed the hungry, give a drink to the thirsty, provide shelter for the stranger, furnish clothes for the naked, visit the sick, and minister to the prison-bound.

It is my prayerful hope that all who read this work will no longer ask the question, "How do we minister to the hungry, thirsty, shelterless, stranger, naked, sick, and prisoners among us?" but will move on to the new questions, "When and where do we get started?"

# Introduction

> When they had finished eating, Jesus said to Simon Peter, "Simon, son of John, do you love me more than these?" "Yes, Lord," he said, "you know that I love you." Jesus said, "Feed my lambs." Again Jesus said, "Simon, son of John, do you truly love me?" He answered, "Yes, Lord, you know that I love you." Jesus said, "Then take care of my sheep." The third time he said, "Simon, son of John, you do love me?" Peter was hurt because Jesus asked him the third time, "Do you love me?" He said, "Lord, you know all things; you know I love you." Jesus said, "Feed my sheep" (John 21:15-17, NIV).

*Do you love Me?* The question that Jesus put to Simon Peter during His postresurrection appearance is the basis for what will follow in this work. How you answer, or leave unanswered, this question will determine the direction your ministry will go in either sacrificial service, self-service, or no service.

Three times Jesus put the question to Simon Peter—"Do you love Me?" And three times Peter responded by saying, "Yes Lord, You know that I love You." The following sequence of this question-and-answer dialogue moves into the area of conscious and concerted action: Feed My sheep! Jesus is saying to Simon Peter and to all the other "Simon Peters," that if your love for

Me is total, unconditional, and undivided, then it must and it will manifest itself in concrete and tangible action. No love, no labor of love; no labor of love, no love.

We, like Simon Peter, are still being addressed by these same postresurrection words of our Lord.

*Do you love me? Then feed My sheep!* Jesus is teaching, telling, turning our perspective from presuppositions and principles and in effect is saying, "Take these and demonstrate them in practice." In fact, the only authentic manifestation that your Christ relationship is genuine will be in the area of applied Christianity. Words alone will not suffice, but both words and work will be sufficient to declare the will of God to a hungry or thirsty "sheep" or one who is sick or prison-bound.

I believe it is necessary at this point to clarify, as we are about to move into the feeding ministry, that I am not proposing or implying that one has to work for salvation. Nothing could be further from the truth as I read the biblical record. I believe salvation is obtained by grace through faith in Jesus Christ, and that it is a gift of God. What I am proposing in this work is that once we have been saved, we will be touched completely in our lives so much that we will want to be obedient to all of our Lord's demands and commands. Jesus said that the scope and depth of our obedience to Him would be in direct measurement to our love for Him (see John 15:10, 14).

And so we return to that haunting, hounding, it-will-not-go-away question: Do you love Me? If you, by some dismal decision, answer "no," then you have just determined your present and eternal destiny without God. But if, just "if," you have and will always answer "yes," then you, by your response, have set the course to show that love in feeding in the sheep.

This feeding of the sheep will be considered in six

areas; namely, the hungry sheep, the thirsty sheep, the sheep who are strangers, the naked sheep, the sick sheep, and the prison-bound sheep.

Since we are sheep ourselves, we will not attempt to write our diet or determine our menu selection. To do this, we will need to consult the sheep manual—the Holy Bible—to find out the what, when, where, why, and how of our feeding.

I pray that you will go with us as we consider further our Lord's demanding words to Simon Peter as He said to them on that postresurrection morning nearly two thousand years ago—"[If] you love Me, . . . feed My sheep!"

Feeding the Sheep

# 1
# Feeding the Hungry

*"For when I was hungry, you gave me food"*
*(Matt. 25:35, NEB).*

## Biblical Perspectives

Jesus, in the before-mentioned text, states quite clearly that one of the responsibilities we have as His disciples is to feed those who are hungry. In fact, as we read the entire context of the text, we understand that it is one of the requirements for our acceptance into His kingdom.

"If a man has enough to live on, and yet when he sees his brother in need shuts up his heart against him, how can it be said that the divine love dwells in him?" (1 John 3:17, NEB). The obvious answer is you cannot say that the divine love dwells in you, have the means to alleviate the needs of those around you, and do nothing about it.

Let us turn to selected passages from the Old Testament and then to the New Testament to see what our Lord has said concerning the feeding of His sheep; and from these Scripture passages, develop a ministry strategy for our contemporary setting.

### Old Testament

"God also said, 'I give you all plants that bear seed everywhere on earth, and every tree bearing fruit which yields seed: they shall be yours for food' " (Gen. 1:29, NEB).

"The Lord God took the man and put him in the garden of Eden to till it and care for it. He told the man, 'You may eat from every tree in the garden, but not from the tree of the knowledge of good and evil; for on the day that you eat from it, you will certainly die' " (Gen. 2:16, NEB).

From these passages in the Genesis narrative, we are taught that our Father God had provided abundantly for the physical necessities of mankind. I am not about to go into a scholarly discussion of trying to determine the origins of these texts. I will leave that to theologians to argue or answer. My concern is to show that from the beginning of humanity (actually before humanity), God had provided abundantly for His creatures. What a thought! Before Adam or Eve ever experienced their first hunger pain, God had sufficiently supplied their needs!

Certainly our God is a Good Shepherd; for He fed, and He feeds His sheep abundantly.

> The Israelites complained to Moses and Aaron in the wilderness and said, "If only we had died at the Lord's hand in Egypt, where we sat around the fleshpots and had plenty of bread to eat! But you have brought us out into this wilderness to let this whole assembly starve to death." The Lord said to Moses, "I will rain down bread from heaven for you. Each day, the people shall go out and gather a day's supply, so that I can put them to the test and see whether they will follow my instructions or not" (Ex. 16:3-4, NEB).

In this account from Exodus, we see the people (sheep) of God as He was leading them out of Egyptian bondage into a Land of Promise, complaining unto the

Lord even though their confrontation was with Moses and Aaron about their not getting three meals and a midnight snack.

The Lord heard their complaining and moved by sending manna, as the Israelites called it, to feed them on a daily basis. It is interesting to read further in this Exodus narrative how each person was to gather just enough to supply the daily need. When they attempted to gather additional amounts for the next day, it became contaminated, and thus, unusable.

There is a profound lesson for us to learn here if we have eyes and ears to see and hear it. We live in a culture that dictates to us to get all we can and can all we get. We would rather dump the surplus on the ground than store it in empty stomachs. We believe that the price and profit makes right more so than the person. How true, but how tragic!

> Be careful that you do not forget the Lord, your God, failing to observe his commands, his laws, and decrees that I am giving you this day. Otherwise, when you eat and are satisfied, when you build fine houses and settle down, when your herds and flocks grow large and your silver and gold increase and all you have is multiplied, then your heart will become proud and you will forget the Lord your God, who brought you out of Egypt, out of the land of slavery. . . . He gave you manna to eat in the desert, something your fathers had never known, to humble and to test you so that in the end it might go well with you (Deut. 8:11-17, NIV).

The word of warning came to the Israelites through God's mouthpiece and messenger Moses. The warning was given to them in the light of a people's posture to forget, once the storm has passed over, who, or what, actually sustained them. The Lord wanted His people to be fully reminded that it was He who had brought them, led them, and fed them.

Two thoughts are paramount to this passage: Do not forget your hunger; do not forget the food I fed you.

Why in the world would the Lord want His people to remember their hunger? We usually try to recall the delicious meal we just ate or plan ahead on what we want to eat the next time, but no one consciously sits down to recollect their memories of their previous hunger. This is exactly what the Lord wanted His people to do. You see, hunger refers to our craving and desirous appetite for food. It is when we can recall clearly and consciously our craving and desiring of food that we can consciously and gratefully recall how our need was met. It was of this that our Lord wanted His people to be fully aware. Just as you crave the physical food, I want you to crave for Me—not just for the physical food that I give, but crave or desire Me.

> Some lost their way in desert wastes;
> they found no road to a city to live in;
> hungry and thirsty, their spirit sank within them.
>
> ......................................................................................
>
> Let them thank the Lord for his enduring love
> and for the marvellous things he has done for men:
> he has satisfied the thirsty
> and filled the hungry with good things (Ps. 107:4-9,
>     NEB).

This psalm tells of God's unlimited, and unchanging love for His people. He has supplied their needs and delivered them according to His graciousness and abundant supply.

Hunger, which is referred to in the psalm, is a real need and an ever-present reality in any community of any people. They may be the redeemed of the Lord or

they may be the rejects of a status-sick society. Be it as
it is, the hungry are present and they will not fade into
the background or go away and not come again.

Verse 6 states that they cried to the Lord in their
troubles and He delivered them from their distress.
Those who are hungry and needy are still crying to the
Lord for bread and deliverance. What is the church's
answer? What is your answer? Jesus gave the answer;
"Feed My sheep."

> If your enemy is hungry, give him bread to eat; and if
> he is thirsty, give him water to drink; so you will heap
> glowing coals on his head, and the Lord will reward you
> (Prov. 25:21-22, NEB).

The context of these words of wisdom is addressed to
one's dealing with an enemy. If you resist your enemy,
or put up a violent response to his violence, you have
simply kept the anger or battle going. If you reverse the
normal response and give love in the place of hate, and
forgiveness in the place of venegance, you work toward
winning your enemy.

The direction is given with a word of promise that
the Lord will reward you. You will be rewarded because of your attitude—not repaying evil for evil—and
you will be rewarded in your action—giving good for
the bad. You will be rewarded in your affirmation—
believing and behaving in accordance with God's will.

Perhaps too many times we look upon those who
need our assistance as our enemy. We see them approaching the door of the church and we attempt to
remove ourselves from their presence or avoid having
to be confronted by them. They ring our doorbells and
we try to give the appearance that we are not at home.
They approach us in the marketplace and we try to
make like we do not see, hear, or smell them. They ask

us for a quarter but we have no change—even though we are on our way to play the video games or to patronize a vending machine for something to eat or drink.

The word of wisdom to such a situation is, if your "enemy" is hungry, give him bread to eat.

> Is it not sharing your food with the hungry,
> taking the homeless poor into your house,
> clothing the naked when you meet them
> and never evading a duty to your kinsfolk?
> Then shall your light break forth like the dawn
> and soon you will grow healthy like a wound newly
>     healed;
>
> .................................................................................................
>
> if you feed the hungry from your own plenty
> and satisfy the needs of the wretched,
> then your light will rise like dawn out of darkness
> and your dusk by like noonday (Isa. 58:7-10, NEB).

False religion and empty worship set the tone for these words of challenge and confrontation. The post-Exilic people of God had returned to their homeland, but instead of majoring in the monumental work of the Lord, they placed their emphasis upon their own welfare. They were undergoing the proper procedures outwardly, but inwardly they were full of folly. Their hands were put forth, but their hearts and heads were not in it.

The Lord spoke to His people by telling them in an instructive way that He will accept only genuine worship of Him. He called for the people to share their food with the hungry, to take the homeless poor into their houses, and not to evade their responsibilities in caring for their kinsfolk.

This is a far cry from our postures of putting forth our hands to help those who are hungry, homeless, and hopeless. Our tendency has been to send them away—up the street to some community center, across town to some social agency. Come back on the next Sunday right after morning services or just before the afternoon or evening services start. Please be cautious and careful not to disturb our full-line program layout.

The word of the Lord to those in Isaiah's day is still the same word to us: Share your food, take in the homeless, feed the hungry from your plenty. The thought is that you do not have to go and get any food or supplies, the Lord has already abundantly provided enough for you and the one in need. We do not need a new means of receiving; we need to apply the old way of distribution.

As with the word in Isaiah, as you do what the Lord has commanded, either as a church, or an individual, there are promises of prosperity. "Then shall your light break forth like the dawn and soon you will grow healthy like a wound newly healed. . . . The Lord will be your guide continually and will satisfy your needs in the shimmering heat" (vv. 8$a$,11$a$).

The opportunities are before us, will we be obedient to our God-given responsibilities?

> Consider the man who is righteous and does what is just and right.
>
> ............................................................................................
>
> He gives bread to the hungry and clothes to those who have none. He never lends either at discount or at interest. He shuns injustice and deals fairly between man and man. He conforms to my statutes and loyally observes my laws. Such a man is righteous; he shall live, says the Lord God (Ezek. 18:5-9, NEB).

"Consider the man [person] who is righteous and does what is right and just." These are the opening

words of the Lord through His mouthpiece Ezekiel.
The Lord says the person who "gives bread to the hungry and clothes to those who have none is a righteous,
right-related person to the Lord. Is this not stimulating?
For we seldom think of being rightly related to the
Lord along with how we release our goods to care and
feed the hungry. We usually think of righteousness in
terms of doctrinal defense rather than daily bread distribution. The Lord states it just the opposite: How you
relate to your brother and sister is a direct indication of
how you are related to Me.

It is also interesting to note in this passage that the
Lord said the righteous man does not lend to receive.
He lends or gives because he loves. His reward is being
able to give. Too often when we do help someone, we
consider what return we will get. If I give, what will I
get back? Will my help be recognized? I need witnesses
to verify that I helped someone. If these are not present
in the immediate situation, I will call up someone to
inform them. I may even have the audacity to remind
the individual continually that I helped them when
they needed it. This is not what the Lord directs us to
do. He tells us to give without any drum rolls or banners
waving. Just do it with the confidence that your Father
knows and sees. Do not do it to receive a reward; if you
do, you will certainly lose it.

A righteous man, states the Lord, is conformed to My
statutes and loyally observes My laws. The idea of con-
formity moves us beyond the "feeling level," where
you and I both have heard regretfully too many times,
I did not give them anything because I did not "feel"
like it. Or I helped them because I "felt" good about it.
The Lord has never instructed us to serve Him or our
fellow brothers and sisters based upon how we *feel*. We
do His work, His way, because He has commanded it of

us, and our love for Him automatically prompts us to respond in love.

### New Testament

> After fasting forty days and forty nights, he was hungry. The tempter came to him and said, "If you are the Son of God, tell these stones to become bread." Jesus answered, "It is written, 'Man does not live on bread alone, but on every word that comes from the mouth of God'" (Matt. 4:2-4, NEB).

After Jesus had been baptized in the Jordan by John the Baptist, after Jesus' identity was clearly stated—"this is my beloved son in whom I am well pleased" (Matt. 3:17, KJV)—it was after the Holy Spirit came in the form of a dove, and after Jesus had been led into the wilderness and fasted for forty days and forty nights that the tempter came to Him and challenged Him to turn rocks into rolls.

Jesus' first temptation was not over doctrine, His teaching, preaching, His political philosophy, or His social ideology. It was not over His community relations program or His new financial system He was about to institute. No, Jesus' first temptation was over hunger and bread. Take this stone and make some sandwiches. Take this dust and make dinner rolls.

Jesus' reply set the standard and the guide for our ministry to those who are hungry. Jesus did not say that persons do not need bread. He said that we do not need bread *alone,* meaning something else must accompany the bread we eat. Humanity is more than an empty stomach which must be filled three times a day, and sometimes with a snack in between or at the end of the day. People need bread; the physical kind which translates into beans, broccoli, beef, and biscuits. We just do not live on these alone. We also need the bread—believing in our Creator, behaving in our relationships with other persons, and beholding the brevity of our lives and the blessings that have been provided through Jesus Christ, our Lord and Savior.

Humanity does need bread; if it were not so, Jesus would not have fed over five thousand persons in Capernaum, sent His disciples into town to buy food as He passed through the Samaritan territory, would not have gone to a meal at Matthew (Levi's) house, ate in Zacchaeus's house, or had table fellowship in Simon's house. In fact, the one major way that Jesus wanted all of His disciples to remember Him was by way of a meal.

As we survey the New Testament, we will look at selected passages of Scriptures that will help us understand better what our God meant and means as He instructs us to feed His sheep.

"Give us this day our daily bread" (Matt. 6:11, KJV). Our Lord instructs us to daily ask the Father, who supplies abundantly, for food and substance as needed.

"As You have given us this day, so give us the bread—the substance that is needed to sustain us." Both the day and the day's supply are given. God does not give life without giving the necessary essentials to sustain that life. Go back and think about the Genesis narrative of Adam. Food and water were provided before Adam was created. All Adam had to do was to tap the resources that were there.

For those of us who live in America, a land of abundant plenty, it seems almost foolish if not downright impractical, to daily make our request to the Lord to supply our bread needs. Even my own children have next month's schedule of what the menu will be in their school cafeteria. I suppose as they look up there and see that the day's offering will be hamburgers or pizzas, they will rejoice; if it's vegetable plates and whole wheat bread, they will regret it.

And yet, be all of this as it is, we are still taught by our Lord to pray for daily substance. This helps both our perspective that God is the sovereign provider and it helps our priorities. He alone is worthy to be praised for His providential care.

> They devoted themselves to the apostles' teaching and to the fellowship, to the breaking of bread and to prayer. Every day they continued to meet together in the temple courts. They broke bread in their homes and ate together with glad and sincere hearts (Acts 2:42,46, NIV).

These few verses give us a look at the agenda of the first-century church—serious study of Jesus' words as He gave them to the apostles, faithful fellowship in forming a family of believers, persistent petitioning prayers of praise, and breaking of bread.

Let's go back and look at that agenda again. Devotion to the apostles teaching—important; fellowship—important; prayer time together—important; and breaking of bread—important. These Christians were not ascetic idealists; they were practical realists, with a hungering for the Bread of Life and yet they knew their needfulness of physical food. They were aware of it, accepted it, and shared together to alleviate it.

The barometer of the spirituality of the Christian fellowship was recorded in their reclining together in table fellowship. "Every day they continued to meet together in the temple courts. They broke bread in their homes and ate together with glad and sincere hearts." Food and fellowship were not separated into false categories of secular and sacred. Bread and blessings were united, so that the blessings of God were made known through the breaking of bread.

As we read further in Acts 4:32-35, we discover that all the believers were one in heart and mind. No one laid claim to anything as their own possession. There were no needy persons among them; for as the need, so was the resource of their freewill collective giving and sharing.

Let us not paint the picture that there were none who were rich or none who were poor. This would confuse us and miss the point completely. Some owned land, and some did not. Some brought much, and some did not have anything to bring. The point is, wherever and whatever the need, it was met.

In almost any society, there will be the haves and the have-nots. In a church community, the haves should be willing to share freely with the have-nots; and not in a condescending or paternalistic manner, but rather as brother to brother, sister to sister.

This author is too well acquainted with churches and church members who have been asked for assistance from one of their sister churches or from one of the members of the fellowship, and it seemed as though boards, committees, congregational meetings had to be called, pastoral approval had to be given, financial reports from both the treasurer and financial secretary had to be given, last year's budget had to be reviewed, this year's budget had to be considered, crystal balls had to be looked into to see the possibility of whether they could or would "pay" it back, and what will be the social or political fallout if we do not help. This kind of action is not only nonsense, it is an abomination in the sight of a just and compassionate God, who lets His rain and sunshine fall and rise on the just and on the unjust.

There is that constant danger that we will search for

a new strategy to do the what, how, when, why, and where of what the Lord wants us to do, rather than studying the Scriptures with the Holy Spirit's guidance to be informed and inspired to carry out the expressed will of God.

> In those days when the number of disciples was increasing, the Grecian Jews among them complained against those of the Aramaic-speaking community because their widows were being overlooked in the daily distribution of food. So the Twelve gathered all the disciples together and said, "It would not be right for us to neglect the ministry of the word of God in order to wait on tables. Brothers, choose seven men from among you who are known to be full of the Spirit and wisdom. We will turn this responsibility over to them and will give our attention to prayer and the ministry of the word" (Acts 6:1-4, NIV).

That hunger and the alleviating of hunger was high on the church's agenda in the first century is apparent from this Scripture passage.

You may want to read a good Bible commentary on the Book of Acts to get a historical and sociological perspective of the context of the text. For our purposes, I am looking at it from the standpoint of the method that was employed to fill empty stomachs.

These Jewish Christians suffered persecution from two major areas at this time. The first was the Roman occupation of their territory which continually caused them to pay exhaustive taxes. The second was the disownership many received when they embraced Jesus as the Messiah; especially when those Jews who did believe in Jesus as the Messiah opened the door to embrace non-Jews, Gentiles, into the same fellowship. Some Bible commentators have pointed out that the reason there was such a large number of widows present at this particular time was that the elderly would make their way to Jerusalem to die in the Holy City; thus, many of their husbands had died leaving them at the mercy of others. Be all of this as it was, the main issue was hunger; the Christian community was sharing what they had to meet this need but a disturbance happened over the unjust distribution.

Several principles should be pondered from this text to get a clearer perspective on how we, today, can administer to those of like condition among us.

First, a systematic procedure of equal distribution of food should be utilized. If the Grecian Jews had been receiving a fair share of what was available, the complaint would not have arisen.

If, within your church, you have (and I pray that you will have, if you do not) a plan or a program of how you want to assist those who are hungry, make sure that it is as just as humanly possible. A stated day of distribution, with time, amount, what is to be distributed, would be a start. Within the area of amount, if you know that you will have only so many baskets or so many plates of food, you may want to announce this, so that when you put up the all-gone sign, some will be sensitive to it.

Second, make sure that your food distributors are just and honest. The apostles knew that those who would be serving in this ministry would be handling money, supplies, and resources. If they were the least dishonest, the whole system would be in worse condition than it was before they were selected. The human posture being what it is, we have a natural tendency to give more assistance to those whom we like. Jesus never said anything to Peter about liking his sheep. He told him, "[if] you love me, feed My sheep."

Third, the pastor or other senior ministers should maintain their identity as preachers of the gospel and not become physical food distributors. When we give someone a loaf of bread or a cold cup of water, we are doing it in the name and obedience to Jesus Christ. It is His lordship that we acknowledge, affirm, and accept —that is why we are doing it. This focus must always be kept clear. The pastor must give spiritual leadership and feed the flock with the Word of God, so they will have the proper nutrients and vitamins to have stamina and strength to be fully obedient to the Lord's commands.

I have known pastors and preachers that have gone to the extreme and gotten over into what is erroneously labeled the "social gospel," while neglecting *the gospel.* If you are preaching the gospel, teaching the gospel, and applying the gospel, it encompasses all of life.

The fourth point is that when the apostles said they would give themselves to prayer and the ministry of the Word, this is not to be understood that they had washed their hands or removed themselves from the area of ministry completely.

For what would they be praying? For God's guidance in this matter and all the other concerns of the Christian community. They would be studying and searching the Scriptures for further insight and direction in this matter of how to feed the sheep and how to nurture and nourish the entire congregation on the Word of God. Once again, it needs to be mentioned that we do not want to get divided in calling one area of ministry sacred and another secular.

> And though I bestow all my goods to feed the poor, and though I give my body to be burned, and have not charity, it profiteth me nothing (1 Cor. 13:3, KJV).

In the thirteenth chapter of 1 Corinthians, we find the fulfilling thought of what Jesus said to Peter in John 21:15-17—*If you love me, feed my sheep.* The text states the supreme standard by which we, too, will be measured—love. This verse shakes and awakens us, that even though we were to give away all that we had, food, clothing, shelter, money, or whatever, it will all be of no profit to us if we did not do it for the love motive.

Many persons will be moved to help feed hungry people, but all will not do it because of the love they have for God or for their fellow persons. Some persons feed the hungry sheep just so they can show those sheep how well off they—the feeders—are, at the expense of showing the hungry how bad a condition they are in themselves. Some help to write off their contribution as tax benefits—an indirect way of giving money to make money. This is shameful, but true. Some give just so they can boast about what they did. They have never read Jesus' words about not letting your left hand know what your right hand is doing. Some give just to be a part of the in crowd. Everyone was asked to give something and since I am a part of the group, I wanted to do my part. In this instance, they care more about the group's approval than the need of the other person. The list is endless as to why some give to others.

The Scripture clearly states to us that any reason, except love, is not acceptable to the Lord.

It was the basis of love that Jesus gave the command to Peter to feed His sheep. It is on this same basis that Paul wrote to the Christians at Corinth. All arguments of superiority, special places of position and rank are canceled by love. If you love, then you will demonstrate it by what you do. "Feed My sheep!"

Remember this! Whoever sows sparingly will also reap

sparingly, and whoever sows generously will also reap generously. Now he who supplies seed to the sower and bread for food will also supply and increase your store of seed and will enlarge the harvest of your righteousness. You will be made rich in every way, so that you can be generous on every occasion; and through us, your generosity will result in thanksgiving to God (2 Cor. 9:6,10-11, NIV).

The selected passage, taken as a whole, is Paul's correspondence with the church at Corinth concerning the anticipated love offering he was to receive from them to take to the saints who were in a desperate situation at Jerusalem.

For our purposes, let us focus upon several factors which can be gotten from the entire ninth chapter.

First, Paul began by writing to them: There is no need for me to write to you to fill in the gaps concerning the need of the saints at Jerusalem, nor is there need for me to "sell" you on the idea of giving to alleviate the need. You know about the situation and you know your means already available to assist them.

This is a good beginning strategy for ministry of a church or for an individual Christian. We waste far too much time in wanting to be brought up-to-date with all the particulars and complete background information. Usually, when a need is verbally expressed in the congregation, many persons knew of it prior to its disclosure.

Second, Paul wrote that he was sending some of the brethren to assist in the final details of how the generous gift they were giving can be finally collected so that the time of reception and distribution to the needy persons could be made just as short as possible.

Another insight that can be derived here is that when the congregation has in mind to give all to the needy, it is time for the pastor or leaders of the flock to give some tangible guidelines as to how best the monies or resources can be accumulated and then distributed.

Third, Paul wrote to remind them that even though they had in mind to give, only what they actually put in the offering plate will be counted and, thusly, used.

We have often heard persons say, "I had a mind to give or do more." Sorry, but we cannot count your mind and we cannot deposit your good intentions at the bank. Just try to write a one-hundred-dollar check with twenty-five dollars worth of good intentions. I hope you get the picture.

Fourth, each person should give what he has decided to give in his heart, not out of compulsion, but out of compassion.

People's arms would not be so twisted if their hearts have been touched. The proportionate side of their giving is emphasized thusly: just in the measure that they give, so it will be measured for them to receive. You have the promise when you give freely, with no compulsion and no strings attached. The Lord, the Supplier of all, will see to it that your abundant increase of what He will give will far exceed what you give. In other words, "You can't beat God giving; the more you give, the more He will give to you."

Fifth, when we give freely for the causes of helping other brothers and sisters, we are not only giving to alleviate their need, but we are also glorifying God. Paul wrote in verse twelve: "This service that you perform is not only supplying the needs of God's people, but is also overflowing in many expressions of thanks to God" (NIV).

Our giving to help others can be a means whereby we witness to the unregenerate that Jesus saves, because He dwells in the lives of His people, and His people go and rescue those who are perishing.

Our confession of the gospel of Christ is made known through expression of generous giving to those in need.

"For even when we were with you, we gave you this rule: 'If a man will not work, he shall not eat' " (2 Thess. 3:10, NEB). This passage needs to be looked at for no other reason than the fact that this author has heard it taken completely out of context and given an interpretation that is not only foreign and incorrect, but dangerous.

Paul was addressing the Christians in Thessalonica, who were awaiting the Lord's return almost instantly. This experience of expectant hopefulness had created a situation where many had ceased to go about their daily tasks of working, earning wages, and maintaining a daily routine. The reason was that they believed Christ's return was upon them.

The situation had developed to the degree that those who could work, who could provide for themselves, were turning to the church for support. It is this issue which the Scripture addresses. There is work to do; there are able, capable persons who can do the work, but they are refusing, looking strictly and solely to the church to care for them.

Paul instructed the leaders to tell those who can work to go to work, provide for themselves and their families, and let not the church be taxed for such. Paul even used the example of himself in working with his own hands to provide for his needs, not because it would have been wrong for the church to compensate him for what he was doing for them spiritually, but he stated he did not accept compensation so none could accuse him of hindering the gospel.

No work, no bread. Yes, if there is work, employ-

ment, with jobs available, capable, able persons ought
to do the work.

Let us look at the other side of this. What about persons who either cannot work because of physical or
mental inability or because of their present job skills?
Often there is no employment for them.

The first group, those who cannot work because of
physical or mental inabilities, must be cared for by
those who can. First, it is the families of these persons
who are to care for them. The Scripture clearly states
this in 1 Timothy 5:4. If there is no family, then it
becomes the responsibility of the church. Notice, I did
not say it is the responsibility of some social agency or
government program, though these certainly can be
used and should be used. I said it was the responsibility
of the church to care for those in like condition. If you
would read the histories of most hospitals, nursing
homes, insurance companies, benevolent organizations, funeral directorships, and cemeteries, you would
discover that these got their start and support from
local churches or church organizations. Somehow,
somewhere, somebody attempted to shift the responsibility of caring for the sick, feeding the hungry, and
sheltering the homeless away from the church to society.

The second consideration is the unemployed. What is
the church's responsibility to them? The Word of God
instructs us to be of the same mind one to another, bear
one another's burdens, weep with them who weep. I
hope you get the picture. The way this could, and
should, work would be quite simple. Just suppose you
had a church membership of five hundred members. If
there were an unemployed person with family responsibilities, each member could give just one dollar per
week—that would be five hundred dollars per week

income. If the person was unable to find work over an entire year, he/she would receive twenty-six thousand dollars a year of "love compensation" from the church family.

Keep in mind that this would be the bare minimum. This does not include additional funds from unemployment benefits, food stamps, insurances, or other sources. Of course, if the church is being obedient to the Lord's command of bringing His tithe and offering into His storehouse, there would already be enough "meat" in the deep freeze to more than adequately meet every need. A church that receives tithes should be a tithing church.

> To the elders among you, I appeal as a fellow elder, a witness of Christ's sufferings and one who also will share in the glory to be revealed: Be shepherds of God's flock that is under your care, serving as overseers—not because you must, but because you are willing, as God wants you to be; not greedy for money, but eager to serve; not lording it over those entrusted to you, but being examples to the flock. And when the Chief Shepherd appears, you will receive the crown of glory that will never fade away (1 Pet. 5:1-4, NIV).

The elders (pastors) were given the appeal by Peter to shepherd the flock under their care. The word *shepherd* is the verb *poimainō* in the Greek, which means *feeding, guiding, leading, and caring for the sheep.* The reason for this pastoral loving care was because of both the present suffering and persecution that the Christians were receiving and because of the future reality that these would increase.

Three reasons are given as to why and how the shepherd is to care for the flock. First, the shepherds are to serve as overseers. They must be the watchmen on the

wall overseeing the condition of the flock. They must
have a perspective that is different from the sheep—
being multifocal—able to look ahead, behind, and
around so that the sheep can be guided in the right
direction and brought into green pastures. Second, the
shepherd (pastor) is to serve as an overseer because of
his willingness to do. One must not take the position by
being constrained. If one is in the position of shepherd
of the flock by constraint, he will remain there only as
long as the constraint restrains him. Third, the shepherd is to be eager to serve. His service is ultimately
unto the Lord, and, thusly, he has real joy in serving
God's flock. Notice I said the sheep are God's flock; they
are not the shepherd's sheep, or the pastor's people.

It is with this basic interpretative understanding that
we can grasp that it is for the pastor to care for the flock
that has been assigned to him. His responsibilities are
to find the method and the means, and then to convey
the message to the flock that there is "food" available
and how they can obtain it.

Pastors serving in the local congregation must be on
the wall, looking out for the total welfare of those who
have been assigned to their care. They must be on the
alert, looking—not just waiting—for someone to come
to them. They must move among their people and go
out into the real world where their sheep graze to discover the circumstances they confront each day.

The shepherd must serve to protect and guide the
sheep. If sheep in his flock are hungry for both physical
and spiritual food, he must, by God's grace, find a way
to feed them. The sheep must be adequately taught
about food purchasing, nutritional health, dietary
guidelines, quantity and quality control. If the sheep
are going to a neighborhood grocery store where the
prices are two, three, or even four times as high as they

are at a larger chain grocery store, means must be worked out to get the sheep into another "grazing field."

If the sheep are receiving food stamps or supplemental income, the shepherd must give a plan to the sheep to show how they can get the best quantity at the most economical price. Buying a ten-ounce box of something when a thirty-two ounce box costs only a dollar more is not wise.

If the sheep are in poor health and most of their health problems can be directly correlated to their improper or incorrect diet, the shepherd must give the sheep a healthy sermon on the connection of gluttony and grief. Too much sugar, too much salt, too much greasy food, too much red meat, too much anything can be detrimental to one's health. You cannot get me to think heavenly thoughts when I have heavy burdens in my lower extremities.

To feed the sheep involves preaching the Word, but it also involves placing the sheep in green pastures, finding the best prices for the food commodities they must purchase, prioritizing their palates to the most nutritional and healthy foods for their stomachs, and placing the sheep besides still waters so they will receive the Shepherd's words.

> Therefore, they are before the throne of God
> and serve him day and night in his temple;
> and he who sits on the throne will spread his tent over
>     them.
> Never again will they hunger;
> never again will they thirst.
> The sun will not beat upon them,
> nor any scorching heat.
> For the Lamb at the center of the
> throne be their shepherd,

he will lead them to springs of living water.
And God will wipe away every tear from their eyes
  (Rev. 7:15-17, NIV).

In this final book of the Bible, we come to the apex of the assurance that God, the Father, and Jesus, the Lamb of God, will shepherd (feed) His own. Their present condition and position might be dismal and fraught with persecution and suffering, but their heads and hearts can remain steadfast in the pure hope that they will be conquerors because the Lamb has conquered.

This is a refreshing and rejuvenating word to all who love the Lord and look for His blessed second coming. We who are earthly undershepherds must do all that is in our power and means (and it does seem at times we must do even more than this) to alleviate the hurting hunger, and the haunting hopelessness that gets a strong hold on the lives of our people.

We must never substitute bread in the sky for bread for the stomach, or try to supplement hunger with hope. If I am physically hungry, you just cannot tell me about beams of heaven; you have to give me some beans and ham hocks, and then I will be ready to sing.

The Scripture speaks, in pointed, picturesque language, of how the Lamb will spread His protective covering as a tent over His own. He will shepherd, shield, and securely sustain them in His strong arms of redemption.

The absoluteness of their victory and completed journey of wandering in the wilderness of want, weariness, and despair is that never again will they hunger, never again will they thirst. There will be complete satisfaction. All normal cravings and desires will be met; for they would have come to their desired haven.

It is because of this assurance that the day of our Lord and of His Christ is rapidly approaching that we work the works of Him who has sent us; for we know that night is coming when no one will be able to work.

We have heard our Master's voice, "Do you love Me?" And we have responded in the affirmative, "Yes, Lord." And so, we move to feed His sheep.

### Guidelines for Ministries to Feed the Hungry

#### A. Church Clusters

Now, about the collection for God's people: Do what I told the Galatian churches to do. On the first day of every week, each one of you should set aside a sum of money in keeping with his income; saving it up, so that when I come no collections will have to be made. Then, when I arrive, I will give letters of introduction to the men you approve and send them with your gift to Jerusalem. If it seems advisable for me to go also, they will accompany me (1 Cor. 16:1-4, NIV).

From this passage of Paul's correspondence to the church at Corinth, we get a biblical principle of churches clustered to meet the needs of others. When and where there is consolidation of church efforts, the two or three are more adequately equipped than just one alone.

The offering which Paul referred to was for the saints at Jerusalem. Various reasons, all of which seem plausible, have been given about the situation in Jerusalem which had necessitated Paul to make financial appeals to other churches. Some of these reasons are: 1) After their conversion to Christianity, many of the Jews would have been ostracized socially and economically; 2) The "experiment in community sharing" described in Acts 2:44-45; and 4:32, 34-35 undoubtedly would have aggravated, though it did not necessarily cause, their poverty; 3) Persistent food shortages in Palestine, because of overpopulation, culminated in the famine of AD 46 in the time of Roman Emperor Claudius (Acts 11:27-30); 4) As the mother church of Christendom, the Jerusalem church was obliged to support a proportionately large number of teachers and probably to provide hospitality for frequent Christian visitors to the Holy city; 5) Jews in Palestine were subject to a crippling twofold taxation—Jewish and Roman. Any or all of these reasons could be the contributing factors, even in our day, as to why the church must reach out to feed the hungry.

There are persons who have become Christians who receive ostracism and rejection from their families and lose the support of their "friends" because of their loyalty to the lordship of Jesus Christ.

There are food shortages that come to bear because of natural calamity and economic deprivation. Unemployment, hospitalization with not enough insurance coverage to pay the expenses, prolonged illnesses, death of a spouse whose income was necessary to maintain daily bread, changes in federal funding to those who rely upon these supplemental monies to survive. All of these can contribute to a famine situation.

Taxation, high interest rates, and financial loan sharks who deceive people in their borrowing and paying policies, can put any individual or family in a deprived situation.

What should the church do to relieve the hunger of persons who can become victims of such predicaments?

The church can use her resources by utilizing and distributing the "meat" in the storehouse to those who have no house or whose cupboard is empty.

Churches can come together and pool their resources. This can be easily done by each participating church in the cluster giving so much per week, month, or year into a central location or to a designated person approved by all the churches. The church cluster could work with members of its ranks to see if there are persons who have expertise in social work or can give financial advice, nutritional advice, or employment possibilities to those who are in need of such.

The church cluster, which would always include two or more churches, could employ a part-time or, if the need warrants it, a full-time person to handle their weekday ministries in this area. The church cluster could select a reputable, charitable organization to assist them in their mission ministry so that there would be as little overlapping as possible.

Clearly, we have from the Scriptures a biblical principle of churches coming together whether they are in Macedonia or Memphis, Jerusalem or Jacksonville, to work in compassionate concert to be obedient to our Master's charge—"Feed My sheep."

> And now, brothers, we want you to know about the grace that God has given the Macedonian churches. Out of the most severe trial, their overflowing joy and their extreme poverty welled up in rich generosity. For I testify that they gave as much as they were able, and even beyond their ability. Entirely on their own, they urgently pleaded with us for the privilege of sharing in this service to the saints. And they did not do as we expected, but they gave themselves first to the Lord and then to us in keeping with God's will (2 Cor. 8:1-5).

This second passage of Scripture is in reference to the first in that the appeal is still being made to the Corinthian Christians to give out of their abundance.

Several factors can be stated from these verses in

further developing the idea of church clusters. Let me list them.

1. Give according to grace.

The Macedonian churches, such as Philippi, Thessalonica, and Berea had given generously because they were fully aware of the graciousness of God's grace. The church cluster concept will work as each participating church understands that it has been blessed to be a blessing unto others.

2. Do *not* give until it hurts—give until it helps.

The Macedonian churches had no large bank accounts or high-interest yielding money-market certificates. They were under persecution and extreme poverty themselves. But they were willing to give what they had. They just had a willing heart and a generous spirit; thusly, they gave with no restraints—trusting God to supply their needs.

3. Freely you have received—freely give.

Entirely on their own, they gave. No compulsion, no complaining, no constraint; they gave compassionately. In fact, if you read the passage again closely, it states that "they urgently pleaded with us for the privilege of sharing in this service to the saints." What a picture! What hearts! Folk were actually making a fuss to give. That's like sitting in a worship service anxious, nervous, and a little upset because no one has called for the offering and you are worried that they might forget to pass the offering plate. Unimaginable? No, these folks had that kind of spirit.

4. Give yourself first—then all other giving becomes easy.

Not only were the Macedonian churches willing to give of their physical substance, they had already given themselves. Their money would be backed up by their muscle. There are individuals and even churches who have a erroneous idea that if I, or we, give some money, our ministry responsibility has been met. Nothing could be further from the truth. If a person is too weak from not eating, you cannot put coins in their hands, you have to hold the cup up to their mouths. You do not take hungry people to the bank; if you do, it should just be long enough to get some money to buy some bread.

### B. Church Fellowship Co-ops

And all that believed were together, and had all things common; And sold their possessions and goods, and parted them to all men, as every man had need (Acts 2:44-45, KJV).

Taking the concept of sharing our substances so that we can serve our suffering brother and sister is evident from the above-mentioned text.

To feed the hungry within our ranks and reach, the church could develop a co-op type of ministry where each member brings nonperishable goods and places them in what could be called God's Pantry or Food for the Fellowship. If *all* in any church fellowship would do just this, there probably would not be enough room to store it. Have you ever noticed that when you ask each person in a group to bring just one dish for a meal there is always enough food and usually too much to even eat? This is based on the principle of sharing and giving, producing an abundant supply.

Other principles and programs the church could develop along this line of shared resources is:

1. Bulk Buying

The church could buy food items in large quantities at the wholesale price and redistribute them to the members at cost for those who can afford it or charge the account to God's goodness for those who cannot.

2. Church Gardens

The church could plant a churchwide garden, and at harvesttime distribute the harvest to those who are in need. For persons of the fellowship who can fruits and vegetables, this could be done as a mission project, making sure there is always "meat" in the storehouse. Teenagers, who are always needing and looking for employment in the summer, could be hired by the church to oversee the entire operation. This would not only feed hungry stomachs, it would feed empty pocketbooks.

## C. Church-Sponsored Community Kitchens

If the need is great enough in the locale, the church could pursue starting a community kitchen. Federal, state, and local resources need to be checked into to see if there are monies that could assist the project. Also, a community needs survey should be taken to determine, as factually as possible, the real need from the perceived needs of the community.

## D. Food Referrals

The church could work out a plan with a restaurant in the area to feed persons who are authorized by the church for meals. This also could be worked out with grocery stores, where a predetermined church food basket would be prepared in advance and given to the authorized person.

## E. Home Economics

My mother is a dietician by profession. She has worked in large metropolitan hospitals, with staffs of other trained professionals, public schools, nursing homes, and, oh yes, in our home as chief food mechanic. In each one of these situations, she has had to teach the patient, student, or persons about the value and importance of good nutritional health. She has had to teach and train her staffs about the importance of quality and quantity and how to get the most out of what you have. At home, I have seen her take leftovers and make them over as a delicious meal.

The church has a ministry to totally feed the whole person. We must feed their minds with the truth of God, feed their hearts with the love of God, feed their souls with the knowledge and power of the Spirit of God, and feed their strength with both spiritual and physical food.

It is through this last feeding with physical food that the church must teach good nutritional health to her members. Improper diet produces an improper desire to love and learn. It also produces the inability to lift someone who has gone astray or just needs a guiding, encouraging hand to show them the way.

It is amazing how frequent and firm the guidelines are given to the people of God concerning their diets. Eternal truths are given through the expression of a meal. Doctrinal disputes arise and are settled concerning the what, when, where, and how of eating. Since this food business is such an important concern in the biblical text, we would be amiss if we did not address the issue head-on with members of the church.

The church needs to offer nutritional health classes. I am aware that a lot of this information is now being given in the schools; but most church members who are middleaged and up have not received it or it has been so long since their exposure to it, it probably has been forgotten. Usage of food, quality and quantity of foods, and storage of foods all need to be presented. For the elderly and persons with health problems, a food specialist may be consulted to give specialized information. Just about every major illness has some specific guidelines concerning the best diet for the ailment.

All of these aforementioned are suggestions and ideas that can work if the people of God respond in the positive to Jesus' plea to the Simon Peters of this world: Do you love Me? Yes, I love You. Then feed My sheep!

In this chapter we have looked at biblical principles for providing a food ministry to feed the sheep. The church must not release her responsibility in this area to any other concern. As we continuously preach the Scriptures, we will gain even more insight as to the why and how of providing a ministry to those who are hungry in our presence.

You may have noticed at the beginning and throughout this chapter no attempt was made to give a definition of hunger. To do so would be the equivalent of trying to teach the chemical dynamics of water to a drowning person.

Jesus, our Lord, never told us to define the hungry anyway; He told us to deliver them by distributing food to them.

## Questions for Future Ministries

1. What can one individual do to feed the hungry?
2. Name some other ways the church might establish a ministry for feeding the hungry.
3. At your weekly or monthly fellowship meals at a church, why not invite guests who cannot return

the invitation? Also, this could be done at family mealtime or special celebrations at home.

4. How might the church work better with existing social agencies in the hunger ministry?

5. What do you do with the hungry person who comes to the church during the morning or evening worship hour?

6. What would be the feasibility of your church hiring a minister of weekday activities, or a Christian social worker to assist in the hunger ministry?

7. Will you pray prayers of provisions for the hungry? Note: A prayer of provision is that the hungry might be fed and that you might be shown the way to give what is needed.

# 2
# Feeding the Thirsty

*"When thirsty, you gave me drink" (Matt. 25:35, NEB).*

Those of us living in the Western Hemisphere may have some difficulty in embracing the full impact and extent of this statement made by Jesus, our Lord and Savior. Those of you who have lived in a desert or have passed through one can probably get a greater sensitivity to just how vital a necessity water is for human life.

Water, especially in our American culture, is plentiful and is provided at every table. You can get a cup of water from fast-food restaurants; any public building must have so many water fountains based upon the square footage. Water, in fact, is so abundant, it is still the only thing in a commercial store that is "free." I say "free" with quotes to emphasize that I am sure, from a business perspective, the cost of the water fountain and supply is included somewhere in the price of the merchandise.

To begin this chapter, allow me to share with you from Henri Daniel-Rops, *Daily Life in the Time of Jesus,* a segment in which he told of the importance of rainfall and water supply for the survival of life in the Holy Land.

The question of water, therefore, is a very serious one in this country with its dry and fissured earth; it was even more serious two thousand years ago, for then the great works that Israel has now undertaken for its solution did not exist. It is not mere chance that the poetic aspect of water has so large a place in the Bible. "A stream bordered with garden water so fresh never came tumbling down from Lebanon," says the lover in the Song of Songs about his beloved; and a very old hymn, preserved in the Book of Numbers, was called "Let the Well Spring Up," and it begins, "Here is the well that was dug by princes"; the chieftains of the host laid it open with the stones they carved (Num. 21:18). Nor is it by chance that the prophet Ezekiel, to emphasize the splendor of the time when the Messiah should come, foretold that a pure river should spring from the heart of the Temple and that it should flow towards the Dead Sea and make it wholesome (Ezek. 47:8); nor that Christ, when He told the woman of Samaria that He was Himself the expected Messiah, should have compared this message of salvation to "the living water" (John 4:10). A great many wells had to be dug to provide the precious liquid for the people, the cattle and the fields, and it had to be also brought with the greatest care from the springs and streams to the villages. All this had already been in existence for a great while in the days of Christ—from the time of the kings, indeed—and the Jews were proud of not having "watered it with their feet" (Deut. 11:10, RSV). But strict rules had to be laid down so that the water should be used reasonably. In each village, there was a "master of the waters." At a given hour, he would open the sluices and the women would come hurrying, their pitchers on their heads.[1]

Another selected reference which deserves our attention comes from Fred H. Wight in *Manners and Customs of Bible Lands.*

One of the first things done for a guest who has been received is to offer him a drink of water. The purpose of this is recognizing him as being worthy of peaceful reception. Thus, to give a drink of water is the simplest way to pledge friendship with a person. When Eliezer, Abraham's servant, sought a welcome, he did so by requesting of the maiden who came to the well to draw water (Gen. 24:17-18), "Give me to drink, I pray thee, a little water of thy pitcher." And when she made answer, "Drink, my lord," it was an indication that he was welcome to be a guest at the nearby home. With this significance attached to a drink of water, the promise of Jesus takes on new meaning (Mark 9:41), "Whosoever shall give you a cup of water to drink in my name, because ye belong to Christ, verily I say unto you, he shall not lose his reward."[2]

It is with these words that we want to search the Scriptures to see what are our responsibilities and our rewards in giving a cup of water in Jesus' name.

### Biblical Perspectives: Old Testament

Then Moses led Israel from the Red Sea and they went into the Desert of Shur. For three days they traveled in the desert without finding water. When they came to Marah, they could not drink its water because it was bitter. (That's why the place is called Marah.) So the people grumbled against Moses, saying, "What are we to drink?" (Ex. 15:22-27, NIV).

This second biblical account we have selected refers to the children of Israel passing through the wilderness. Three major themes of providential care are dealt with during this pilgrimage. Thirst, hunger, and despair; these three comprise the basic necessities that the people constantly complain about to the Lord.

It is somewhat ironic that the major obstacle that had to be overcome as they left Egypt, the waters of the

Red Sea, became the main element they cried out for
as they passed through the wilderness.

It is also interesting to note that the people cried out
against Moses. They had cried out to the Lord while
they were under the heavy taskmasters in Egyptian
bondage, but now their complaint comes to Moses.

"What are we to drink?" This was the question on
their agenda. Notice the question was not asked, "How
will the Lord solve this situation?"; "What does the
Lord want us to do?"; "Should we go and ask the Lord
for direction to find water?"; not even, "Let us see what
we can figure out." None of these questions were presented; just a simple—"What are we to drink?"

When we encounter persons in their wildernesses,
they, too, ask the simple, straightforward question,
"What are we to drink?" Their cravings for physical
survival have made them unconscious of the divine
provisions. We, too often as Christians in the family of
God who have called and chosen to bring glory to God's
name, take on the attitude and action of these Israelites
crying in the wilderness. We can easily sing about showers of blessings and rivers of joy, but find it far too
difficult to give a needy person a cup of cold water in
Jesus' name. We, like the Israelites in the text, forget
and, thusly, forfeit our faith in our God who can supply
every need.

To thirst is to crave, to desire, to yearn for water, to
be relieved of the arid, dry, feeling that comes with not
having a sufficient supply of water. There are many
thirsty people around us. They are craving for a drink;
some want water for physical refreshment, some want
alcoholic beverages to combat mental anguish, some
want sociability to combat alienation and isolation; and
they are all asking the same question with situational
differences—"What are we to drink?"

The solution to this "drink problem" comes in verse 25. The people cried to Moses and Moses cried unto the Lord. When Moses did this, the Lord showed him a tree; a piece of wood which, when he threw it into the water, made the bitter water sweet. Burdens are always turned into blessings when we behold God, believe in God, and behave according to God's will. Can you just imagine what might have happened if Moses had refused to do as he was told? A close speculation is that they were about to stone him. You do not give people who have been in the desert, dying of thirst, a lecture on the theorectical ramifications of water as a necessary liquid; you give them water.

Do you see the thirsty people in your community who are in their wilderness, down at their Marahs? If you do, what are you waiting for? The same God who showed Moses how to turn bitter waters into blessed sweet water is the same today.

Now there was no water for the community, and the people gathered in opposition to Moses and Aaron. The Lord said to Moses, "Take the staff, and you and your brother Aaron gather the assembly together. Speak to that rock before their eyes and it will pour out its water. You will bring water out of the rock for the community so they and their livestock can drink."

He and Aaron gathered the assembly together in front of the rock and Moses said to them, "Listen, you rebels, must we bring you water out of this rock?" Then Moses raised his arm and struck the rock twice with his staff. Water gushed out, and the community and their livestock drank.

But the Lord said to Moses and Aaron, "Because you did not trust in me enough to honor me as holy in the sight of the Israelites, you will not bring this community into the land I give them" (Num. 20:2,10-12, NIV).

In this section, we learn some positive lessons through the negative attitude and actions of Moses. When a person asks for a cup of cold water, how should you respond?

There three things from this text that you should do and four things that you should not do. Let's consider what you should do.

*First, acknowledge the people.* The whole assembly gathered against Moses and Aaron. Neither Moses or Aaron attempted to pretend that the people were not there. As simple as this must sound, there have been many ministry opportunities where those who could have helped simply tried to pretend the person was not there; and, thusly, concluded nothing needed to be done. Just think about some of the wealthy, prestigious congregations which publicly boast of their foreign mission offerings to a land and people whom they have not seen, and yet would have a real problem going across the tracks or into public housing projects. They do not mean to consciously neglect these thirsty people, they just do not acknowledge them—they are the invisible visible.

*Second, accept the need as genuine and authentic.* This is what Moses and Aaron did. In fact, they realized just how pressing the issue was; they went from the presence of the assembly unto the door of the tabernacle and fell upon their faces. They did not just look at the situation and say, "Oh well, the people are a little thirsty, they will swallow a couple of times and it will go away." No, they were so aware of the need, they took it before God's presence.

When was the last time you saw a thirsty man or

woman and you realized the need was so great and the
problem so serious that you took it before the whole
church, falling down on your knees before the Lord? If
you have not, it is not because there are not any thirsty
people around. Could it be because you have refused to
accept them?

*Third, affirm that there is an answer to the question,
a solution to the problem, even though you may not
have it.* This is what Aaron and Moses did when they
presented the situation before the Lord. Just because
you do not see the way does not mean there is no way;
it simply means you do not see it.

Now let's consider what you should *not* do after you
see thirsty people.

The first thing not to do is to fuss at them because of
their situation. In verse 10, Moses called the community together, but he did so harshly. Listen, take note, get
a hold of this—his attitude was one of contempt for
their situation. It is almost as if he was saying "you have
no right to be thirsty."

Do not curse the people because of their thirst. It is
bad to fuss at the people; it is worse to curse them, for
in cursing someone, you are rejecting them, calling
them something that they are not. Moses forgot, as we
often forget, these were God's people; they were not
Moses' people. It was the Lord's responsibility to care
for His people, to provide and protect them. It was
Moses' responsibility to respond to what the Lord wanted him to do.

To believe that you are the solution would be a third
point to forget. Once again, Moses stated, "Must we
bring you water out of this rock?" No, Moses, neither
you nor Aaron can bring water out of the rock, but God
can. Moses was to be the water boy, not the water
maker.

You may recall in John 6:8-9, that Andrew, Simon Peter's brother, told Jesus, when asked about the provisions that were available, "There is a lad here, which hath five barley loaves, and two small fishes: but what are they among so many?" (KJV). Andrew thought somehow he was to be a part of the solution. Jesus would do the feeding, Andrew was to do the serving.

And, finally, we learn to make sure we are obedient to the method and way of doing what the Lord has told us. In verse 8, the Lord told Moses to speak to the rock and the water would come forth. In verse 11, we see Moses hitting the rock two times. God did not tell Moses to hit the rock; He told him to speak to the rock. Moses' faith failed because he did not believe nor do as he was told. The water came from the rock not because of speaking or striking it, the water came because God is sovereign and in control. He wants our unwavering obedience and loyalty. It was because of this incident of disobedience that Moses' was permitted to see over into the Promised Land, but was not permitted to enter it. What a price for disobedience! "The wages of sin is death; but the gift of God is eternal life through Jesus Christ our Lord" (Rom. 6:23, KJV).

> Then Eliphaz, the Temanite, replied: Can a man be of benefit to God? Can even a wise man benefit him? What pleasure would it give the Almighty if you were righteous? What would he gain if your ways were blameless?
>
> Is it for your piety that he rebukes you and brings charges against you? Is not your wickedness great? Are not your sins endless? You demanded security from your brothers for no reason, you stripped men of their clothing, leaving them naked. You gave no water to the weary and you withheld food from the hungry, though

you were a powerful man, owning land—and an hon-
ored man, living on it.
And you sent widows away empty-handed and broke
the strength of the fatherless. That is why snares are all
around you, why sudden peril terrifies you, why it is so
dark you cannot see, and why a flood of water covers
you (Job 22:1-11, NIV).

These words of Eliphaz were directed to Job. They
were injurious and insulting to Job because he had done
none of the things Eliphaz stated that he had done. It
was Eliphaz's way of writing his law of divine retribu-
tion on Job's case. That law briefly meant God is just—
do the just and right thing and you will prosper and
receive a blessing. Do the wrong or evil thing, and
condemnation and rejection will surely follow. This
concept did not work out because in Job's case, he had
not done any of the things Eliphaz brought against him.

For our purposes, let us look at the passage from the
perspective that we are Job and we have done the
things Eliphaz mentioned against us. For this imagina-
tive reflection, let's say the guilty Job is the First Baptist
Church, in No Compassion County, Refusing to Minister State, Prosperous and Plenty Country.

The First Baptist Church was doing quite well, or
though it seemed, until this fella Eliphaz showed up
one Sunday morning during the worship services.
When recognition of visitors was made, he asked to
speak; and, permission granted, he spoke, and did he
ever speak!

Listen to what He said that Sunday morning (our
pledge Sunday) with a packed house.

"The Lord rebukes you because of your piety and He
brings these charges against you" (v. 4, author).

First Charge:      "Your wickedness is great.

| | |
|---|---|
| Second Charge: | "Your sins are endless. |
| Third Charge: | "Without due cause, you take a brother in pledge," |
| Fourth Charge: | "You strip men of their clothes and leave them naked." You know your inflated interest rates on your goods, your swiftness to evict someone because they are a day behind in their rent, your requirement of collateral on even small loans. |
| Fifth Charge: | "When a man is weary, you give him no water to drink and you refuse bread to the hungry." You have Wednesday night suppers, covered-dish potlucks, anniversary meals, receptions, teas, coffee and doughnuts in the reception area, print the menu two weeks in advance, but you never invite those who cannot return the invitation; you say it's for all, but when I come in the door, some of your strong men and sassy women quickly have me escorted out the door. Why do you do that? |
| Sixth Charge: | "Is the earth, then, the preserve of the strong and a domain for the favoured few?" You look upon me with contempt as though to tell me not only to go away, but that |

I have no right to be, belong, or become.

Seventh Charge: "Widows you have sent away empty-handed and orphans you have struck defenceless" (vv. 7-9, NEB). Surely, in the course of your well-constructed curriculum for Christian education, you have read and studied Exodus 22:21-24. "You shall not wrong an alien or be hard upon him; you were yourselves aliens in Egypt. You shall not ill-treat any widow or fatherless child. If you do, be sure that I will listen if they appeal to me; my anger will be raised and I will kill you with the sword; your own wives shall become widows and your children fatherless" (NEB). Without a doubt, you have read these things. Do you believe it; do you practice it?

Having spoken his piece, Eliphaz leaves the sanctuary, and everyone gives a sigh of relief at his departure.

The next hymn is "Oh, How I Love Jesus." The music comes out of my lips, but the message must come out of my life.

As the deer pants for streams of water,
so my soul pants for you, O God.
My soul thirsts for God, for the living God.
When can I go and meet with God? (Ps. 42:1-2, NIV).

In this passage, we have the yearning of a worshiper in exile who desires to be reunited in the cultic and

festive worship experiences of the Temple. He is so
desirous of this union and the opportunity to give his
uplifted voice to the rejoicing of the worship partici-
pants that he describes it in beautiful and meaningful
simile.

The imagery is almost self-explanatory as the deer,
who has grown arid, dry, dusty, and despondent in his
search for the water hole to refresh, revive, and restore
his strength and maintain the needed balance for his
survival, so the writer of this psalm states in like fashion.
My soul longs for that refreshing, reconciling, and
rehabilitating audience with my God.

If we would take off our "water masks," the desperate cries of brothers and sisters all around us would be
heard, and the serious and sensitive effort to minister to
them would issue out from our compassionate hearts.

We could see the thirsty ones, not just in the desert
but those who are down the street, those whose brooks
have dried up and whose streams have ceased to flow.
If we would only listen, we could hear their moans and
groans, the anguish of anxiety, and the emptiness of
alienation that comes when there are oceans and seas
all around, but no water to drink. We would be moved
to minister when we see those who are crying and they
know not why.

To help a thirsty individual, whatever may have
caused his or her thirst, be it economic insufficiency,
family fallout, mental anguish, social rejection, religion
without right relationship with God and fellow person,
or whatever, we must offer them the living God. Read
again, "My soul thirsts for God, for the living God."
Have we been too quick to talk about the living God
and, yet, in our deeds presented a dead God? We will
pray the Lord can make a way, and yet, when a person
needs help—thirsty if you please—we minister as

though there is no way. We speak trust in the Lord, we act as though the only sufficient trust is a trust fund. We speak love, but we show little compassion.

The living God needs living persons who will offer up their bodies a living sacrifice, holy and pleasing to God, which is their spiritual worship (see Rom. 12:1). A thirsty man or woman needs to know that Jesus is a well springing up into everlasting life, but you must put the physical water in him or her. Too often our ministry model has been Jesus as the well of eternal life. If you are thirsty, just see Jesus and you will no longer be thirsty. This is true if, by it, we mean Jesus is the One, the only One, who can satisfy and fulfill our ultimate yearning for communion with God the Father, and lead us into the kind of life that is of substance and eternal in its scope. But you do not minister to physically thirsty individuals by telling them that Jesus is the well of everlasting waters without giving them a cold cup of water in Jesus' name. This cup of cold water can be whatever is necessary to restore, revive, and reconcile them back into the Father's family as a whole person.

Does your soul pant for the "water brooks," does it thirst for the living God? If it does, then hear the words of our Lord anew and afresh—"Feed My sheep!"

> If your enemy is hungry, give him food to eat;
> if he is thirsty, give him water to drink.
> In doing this, you will heap burning coals on his head,
> and the Lord will reward you (Prov. 25:21-22, NIV).

This passage selected from the Wisdom Literature refers to the practical procedure that is to be taken in dealing with a person who is your enemy. If the person has offended you and you go to offend them, then you have created the atmosphere for the escalation of the hostilities. But if, on the other hand, you move toward your enemy with reconciliation as your main objective, you can, by God's help, bring about a restitution.

Notice the care you are to give even to one who is labeled as your enemy. Even though the person may be your enemy, you have a moral responsibility to minister unto them. Nowhere does the Lord give us a command or directive that states, if another person is your enemy, you are free and released from any and all responsibility for their welfare. In fact, as you read the biblical record, just the opposite is true.

If your enemy, not just your family member, friends, or those with whom you are familiar, but if your *enemy* is hungry, give him food to eat; if he is thirsty, give him water to drink.

In so doing, the Scriptures teach that you will be heaping burning coals on his head. A reference which goes back to Leviticus 16:12, where on the Day of Atonement, the high priest would take his censer and fill it with coals of fire and then put the incense upon it to be a sweet smelling savour. The basic thought behind this is that atonement and restitution was being made for the sins of the people. In like fashion, when we offer food or drink to our enemies, we are offering a sacrifice of love that can be the means of reconciliation.

In every metropolitan community of this country, there are transient persons who are viewed by the affluent with contempt. They are looked upon and treated as the enemy. The policeman spots them and either arrests them for loitering or removes them from Main Street. The shop owners spot them and quickly rush to make sure they do not come in or remain around their businesses. They are seen as the enemy to their financial profit. They are spotted in the doorways of public buildings, civic centers, community gatherings, and al-

ways they are looked upon and lifted away as the enemy. They show up at parades without permits, they
come to city parks without picnic baskets, and they go
to social gatherings without invitations.

There is a solution for these socially rejected individuals; there is a peace treaty that can be made; and
an amnesty that can be declared—*feed the hungry and
give water to the thirsty.*

I wonder if business persons, shop owners in downtown business districts have realized the great profit
there would be if they would pool their resources to
provide some type of food and drink for those who are
surrounding them every day. The profits they would
reap would not only show up on their financial ledger
sheets at the end of the month, but their influence of
goodwill would affect the whole community. They
would receive what the Lord has said in His Word—a
reward.

Almost every church that is located in the inner city
or in a downtown business district is constantly being
asked for "handouts" from transient persons, those who
have more hunger than food, more thirst than water.
What we must do as church persons is not to treat these
persons as enemies, but as people whom our Lord
came, suffered, died, and rose for. We must not try so
much to give them "handouts" but rather give them a
"help-up" by our compassionate hearts, willing to minister unto those who are the least among us.

If we give food to the hungry and water to thirsty, we
have the assurance that the Lord will reward.

> The poor and the needy search for water,
> but there is none;
> their tongues are parched with thirst.
> But I the Lord will answer them;

I, the God of Israel, will not forsake them.
I will make rivers flow on barren heights,
and springs within the valleys.
I will turn the desert into pools of water,
and the parched ground into springs.
I will put in the desert
the cedar and the acacia, the myrtle and the olive.
I will set pines in the wasteland,
the fir and cypress together,
so that people may see and know,
may consider and understand,
that the hand of the Lord has done this,
that the Holy One of Israel has created it (Isa. 41:17-20,
    NIV).

This passage historically refers to the children of Israel while they were in Exile in Babylon. They needed the assurance that they were still God's elect people even though their transgression and iniquity had led to their present situation of bondage.

The Syrian desert is the one referred to that would have to be crossed. God did not say that He would reroute them so they would not have to cross it; He gave them the assurance that when they had exhausted their search for water, "I the Lord . . . will make rivers flow on barren heights, and springs within the valleys." God's providential care was to be so inclusive that the trees for protection, food, and health would be there to provide them a safe passageway on their journey.

This word of the Lord speaks to us who seriously seek a way to serve a cup of cold water to those in their own deserts so that God has not forsaken them; they are not the forgotten fold that this world tries to make of them. Those who cry upward and outward will be heard by the listening ears of our compassionate God. The Lord

states in His Word, "I will answer them; . . . I will not
forsake them."

Springs and wells, and flowing fountains and water
faucets will come forth out of the desert. This is a word
of assurance.

To those of us who minister to our Lord's name, we
could seek and find the water holes if we would but ask
the spring of Eternal Water. The Lord wills to relieve
the oppression of His people, to restore the downtrodden, to redeem those in bondage. When we do this
water service, we are working in symphony with the
Lord of life.

I challenge you, this day, to go into the desert where
you live and look with sensitive eyes to see those who
are perishing with thirst—the poor and the needy
whose tongues are parched with thirst.

Somebody needs a cup of water, somebody needs a
cup of soup, somebody needs a cup of hope, somebody
needs a cup of compassion, somebody needs a cup of
direction, somebody just needs a cup.

Do all of this so the people may see and know, may
consider and understand, that the hand of the Lord has
done this, that the Holy One of Israel has created it.

My people have committed two sins:
They have forsaken me,
the spring of living water,
and have dug their own cisterns,
broken cisterns that can hold no water (Jer. 2:13, NIV).

This word of the Lord concerning His stubborn and
rebellious people is described with a water analogy.
The Lord said that His people had committed two sins,
both in the context of water usage. The first, they had
forsaken God, the Fountain of Living Waters. Whenever a person, a church, or a nation goes from the

Source of substance, strength, and sufficiency, it must surely fall. Too often the church has been guilty of forsaking her Lord for the ministry methods of the world or has compromised with community concessions. We must learn anew how to trust God to totally supply all of our needs, always believing that He can, and will, show us the way. When we rely upon the Living Water, we can be assured that we will preach and teach a Living Word, minister a life-changing service, and help a lifeless individual to be restored.

The second sin the people were guilty of committing was: they had dug their own cisterns, broken cisterns that could hold no water. How tragic; water was desperately needed, water was abundantly supplied; but there was no adequate container to receive the water.

Many churches and ministerial programs are ineffective today because they have dug their own cisterns. They have built and geared their ministry programs based upon their own blueprints rather than the Word of God. They look good, but have not let their light shine. There are padded pews, but you cannot find a mercy seat in the house. There are stained-glass windows, but no one has experienced the cleansing power of the blood of Jesus to wash and make them whole. What does your church do when a thirsty person comes to your doors and you have just finished singing "There Shall Be Showers of Blessing"? Your finance committee just reported that the goal has been reached and exceeded by a few thousand dollars and then a thirsty person asks if there is any water in the fountain. Does your fountain flow or does it suddenly spring a leak or dry up?

"My people have committed two sins," said the Lord. Let us, by His grace, commit one righteous act and return to Him as the Fountain of Living Waters.

"But let justice roll down like waters,/and righteousness like an ever-flowing stream" (Amos 5:24, RSV). To a people who were caught up in the pomp and pageantry of ritualistic religion and holy day observances, the Lord spoke through His prophet Amos and told him to tell the people to take away the noise from His ears, and stop burning the sacrifices and incense for they stank in His nostrils. Can you just imagine a beautiful new million dollar-plus sanctuary is to be dedicated, the choir has on new choir robes, an orchestra of sacred music ready to play, all of the big dignitaries, the bigwigs with the big wheels out front, white marble pulpit, new carpet, and freshly cut flowers upon the altar, and in walks this prophet from Tekoa with the smell of sycamore on him and tells everybody present that the Lord has told him to tell you—all this stinks!

What would your reaction be? Where would you go for a refuge; what would you do to remedy the situation? It is this last question that confronts and challenges us to reexamine ourselves and our ministry.

What the Lord requires of us is to do justice, and do it so abundantly that it comes down like water, hitting everything, everywhere, at all times. Our right relationship with God our Father must be acted out with our fellow persons as brothers and sisters. Let this righteousness be as a mighty stream. It is to overflow the prescribed boundaries at many points, going beyond what the cruel or carnal law said to do, and moving to the area of ministering until it helps. A mighty stream of righteousness cannot be halted or pushed back. At worst, it will be redirected through another channel; at best, it will flow to its desired end.

What do you say to a thirsty person; what do you do? You tell him or her Jesus is the Well of Everlasting Waters, and show it by giving them a cup of cold water.

## New Testament Perspective

Several passages from the New Testament can help us understand more clearly what our Lord meant when He said, "Inasmuch as you have done it unto the least of these my brethren, you have done it unto me" (Matt. 25:40, KJV). What does it mean to give a cup of cold water in Jesus' name? Why is it important? How do you water thirsty sheep? It is to these questions that we now focus our attention.

> He who receives you, receives me; and he who receives me, receives the one who sent me. Anyone who receives a prophet because he is a prophet will receive a prophet's reward, and anyone who receives a righteous man because he is a righteous man will receive a righteous man's reward. And if anyone gives a cup of cold water to one of these little ones because he is my disciple, I tell you the truth, he will certainly not lose his reward (Matt. 10:40-42, NIV).

These words come at the conclusion of chapter 10 of Matthew where Jesus had called the twelve disciples, commanded and commissioned them for their disciple ministry, informing them of the persecutions that surely would come, and telling them of the undivided allegiance they must have to His lordship if they were to be faithful and, thus, successful.

At the close of these Kingdom instructions, Jesus told them that whoever receives a prophet, a righteous man, or disciple because they represent Him will in no wise lose his reward.

The basic thrust of this passage for us has to do with the evidence of relationship we have to God our Father. If that relationship is authentic, it will show itself in our relationships of accepting those who come to us in our Lord's name and on His behalf. The thought

holds equally true if we accept God as our Father and
Jesus as our Lord and Savior, we will manifest this by
doing good deeds to and for His disciples. Our relationship with God must always be expressed through our
relationship with each other. The little ones of the passage are not to be confused with little children, but
rather, it is to be understood as the people who are
considered "small," of little significance; the ordinary,
everyday people. Jesus is saying to us in this passage
that it is how we treat, how we minister, or fail to
minister, to the "little ones" among us that really is the
determing factor of the depth of our spirituality.

It is not just through the singing of "There Shall Be
Showers of Blessings," or "There Is a Fountain," that
gets our Father's attention and approval; it is through
the giving of a cup of cold water to these "little ones"—
"Inasmuch as you have done it . . . unto Me."

The word comes with assurance if we feed (water)
the sheep, we have the promise that we will not lose
our reward. If we give in Jesus' name, we will get; if we
try to keep, we will lose.

Just look around you my brother and sister. If your
eyes are not too big, you should have no problem seeing
some of these little ones.

> Then he turned toward the woman and said to Simon,
> "Do you see this woman? I came into your house. You
> did not give me any water for my feet, but she wet my
> feet with her tears and wiped them with her hair. You
> did not give me a kiss, but this woman, from the time
> I entered, has not stopped kissing my feet. You did not
> put oil on my head, but she has poured perfume on my
> feet. Therefore, I tell you, her many sins have been
> forgiven—for she loved much. But he who has been
> forgiven little, loves little (Luke 7:44-47, NIV)."

The major ministry principle for us to grasp from this passage is that we will have a free and abundant spirit to minister unto Jesus in a direct relationship as to how we appropriate His gracious goodness to us who are sinners deserving of our condemnation, but, instead, receive His acceptance. This woman in Simon the Pharisee's house had no problem in taking what had been labeled expensive perfume and pouring it out on Jesus. For the precious ointment to her was not in the alabaster box, it was in her grateful heart for what Jesus had done for her.

We in the church are too often like Simon the Pharisee with Jesus in *our* churches; failing to remember that He is in His church and that we ought to receive Him with gratefulness and gratitude. We are in a position to minister only after we have some sense of what the Lord has done for us in spite of us. We all have been in the desert perishing without water, but God, through His grace, has appeared as an oasis in Jesus Christ. We have drunk deeply and freely from Him, the well of eternal waters. Our ministry responsibility now is to give deeply and freely as He has done unto us. Jesus says, if we love much, we will give much. Of course, the opposite of this is tragically true; if we love little, we will give and do little. Could this be why Jesus asked Peter, "Do you love me more than these?" (John 21:15, RSV).

Peter's love for his Lord would be in direct relationship to his service to others. It was true for Peter, and it is true for us. Do you love Jesus? If so, feed His sheep.

> So he called to him, "Father Abraham, have pity on me and send Lazarus to dip the tip of his finger in water and cool my tongue, because I am in agony in this fire (Luke 16:24, NIV).

To get the total insight and impact of this passage,

you must read the entire parable which Jesus gave in
Luke 16:19-31. The basic point of discovery in this parable is that the rich man, in shutting out the beggar
Lazarus, was, in reality, shutting out God from his presence. The rich man was a professing religionist; and,
yet, at the same time, a practical atheist. The rich man
would not have thought of himself as being immoral or
irreligious. He obeyed the Law, kept the Commandments, but had no compassion. He not only did not see
Lazarus as a brother in need, he just refused to see
Lazarus, period.

In this life, we can all attest that there is a great gulf
or division between the haves and the have-nots.
What's so alarming is that this situation can coexist
among persons professing to be children of the King.
Many persons can belong to the same church fellowship, know of the needs of others, have the means and
resources to help or completely alleviate their need,
but go on as though they are nonexisting persons. The
rich man had gallons of "water"; all the beggar needed
was just a "cup." We must be on the constant alert that
we are not "religious" without being redemptive in our
relationships with brothers and sisters who sit at our
gates every day. This author has attended far too many
churches where there have been Spirit-filled worship
experiences, tons of money received, fervent prayers,
and soul-stirring messages have been preached, and
then when Brother Lazarus or Sister Lazarus have
shown up after the benediction, the story was told to
them: "We do not have any bread or water for you."

Jesus is telling us in this parable that there is a payday
coming for those who forget or overlook the Lazaruses
in this world.

May we pray to the Lord of the judgment that we be

found faithful now, giving cups of cold water wherever and to whomever we can.

"When a Samaritan woman came to draw water, Jesus said to her, 'Will you give me a drink?' " (John 4:7, NIV). The first forty-two verses of John 4 gives us six ministry strategies of how to feed the thirsty.

*The first is incarnation—being there in a flesh-and-blood person.* In verse 5—"So he came to a town in Samaria called Sychar, near the plot of ground Jacob had given to his son Joseph." The whole encounter between Jesus and the woman of Samaria would have never taken place unless Jesus had appeared in His fleshly presence.

If we seriously seek a way of ministry unto the thirsty persons around us, there can be no substitute for showing up in person. Remote control will not work.

*The second strategy is an invitation.* "Jesus said to her, 'Will you give me a drink?' " (v. 7). Jesus took the initial move by asking the woman for a drink of water. He saw both her need and His need. His need was to put a well of eternal water in her and to be physically refreshed. Her need at the initial point of contact was to simply receive physical water; later her deep need of spiritual refreshing would be met.

As a ministry principle, we must be where the thirsty are, offer them water (the wet, physical kind), and then move on to the deep level to raise the watermark of their souls. It is not a matter of one without the other; it is a both/and situation. Physical water is important and spiritual water is needed.

*Third—infiltrate boundaries.* In verse 9, the Samaritan woman said to Him, "You are a Jew and I am a Samaritan woman. How can you ask me for a drink?" (NIV).

There are thirsty people all around who are perishing

because of lack of water and we are rejecting them because we see ourselves as "Jews" and them as "Samaritans." These false boundaries and lines of demarcation must be removed and dissolved. There are church fellowships who will tell you very proudly that they help only their own members. There are situations where denominational distinctives are held up as more important than person-meeting-person at the need level.

*Fourth—give information.* In verse 10, "Jesus answered her, 'If you knew the gift of God and who it is that asks you for a drink, you would have asked him and he would have given you living water' " (NIV).

There is the key to the whole scenario—"If you knew the gift of God." Ignorance can only be overcome by information. The Samaritan woman was letting her prejudices and hangups get in the way of her receiving the precious gift of salvation. Think about it, she was thirsty and yet, momentarily, she was letting ethnic differences divide her from a well, springing up into eternal life. How tragic, but how true!

There are thirsty people wandering our streets, thirsty, hungry, homeless, and penniless; all needing some type of help. And yet, there are those cases and situations where help is available and offered, and they refuse because of ignorance.

Give a cup of cold water in Jesus' name but be sure to take the string off the cup when you do it. Simply give the water and present Jesus Christ as the Eternal Spring that is more than sufficient.

*Fifth—insist on ministering.* In verse 13 and 14, Jesus answered,

> "Everyone who drinks this water will be thirsty again,
> but whoever drinks the water I give him will never

thirst. Indeed the water I give him will become in him a spring of water welling up to eternal life."

Jesus could have easily said to the woman, since you have social, sexual, and religious hang-ups about Me, let's just forget the whole matter. Thank God that He does not. He, being the Good Shepherd, saw this woman as a dry, arid, thirsty sheep whose only hope of redemption and refreshment would be through His gracious offer. Jesus insisted, out of love for her.

If we are going to minister effectively in this ministry of feeding the sheep, we are going to need to be insistent. There will come those times when help is available, help is needed, but help will be refused. The depth of our love will be the depth to which we will go to alleviate the aridness of people's lives.

*The sixth ministry strategy is to give insight.* In verses 25 and 26, "The woman said, 'I know that Messiah' (called Christ) 'is coming. When he comes, he will explain everything to us.' " "Then Jesus declared, 'I who speak to you am he' " (NIV).

The thirsty must be enlightened and enlivened to the reality that our God is a God of love who cares about those who would be classified as the least among us. They must be told through the showing of our compassion that it is Father's will that none should perish. Jesus appears in a bold and blessed demonstration every time one of His followers gives a cup of cold water in His name.

As we close this chapter, let us consider briefly two passages from Revelation that speak of the eschatological hope, when all of the sheep will be watered.

He said to me: "It is done; I am the Alpha and the Omega, the Beginning and the End. To him who is thirsty, I will give to drink without cost from the spring of the water of life" (Rev. 21:6, NIV).

There is a reason for our perserverance and pressing toward the day of final redemption; for all those who are thirsting will be refreshed freely from the spring of the water of life. We can serve others because we have been served and we will be served. It is with this faith that we put our servant uniforms on each morning, knowing that our labor is not in vain in the Lord.

> The Spirit and the bride say, "Come!" And let him who hears say, "Come!" Whoever is thirsty, let him come; and whoever wishes, let him take the free gift of the water of life (Rev. 22:17, NIV).

This passage, like the preceding one, speaks of the final day of redemption and restoration. Our ministry task is to go on a seek-and-search mission until we have found the thirsty persons informed, invited, infiltrated, and insisted that they come to Jesus Christ, the well that springs up into eternal life.

Let us be restless until we, by God's grace, rescue the perishing and care for the dying.

Jesus says, "Do you love Me?"; then, "Feed My sheep."

# 3
# Feeding the Stranger

In this chapter, we will look at biblical passages from both the Old and New Testaments to get biblical principles from which to develop ministry strategies for feeding the sheep who are known as aliens, strangers, foreigners, transients, homeless, the fatherless, and the widows.

In every metropolitan area, there is the concern of what to do with the "street people," the roaming transients who seem to pop up almost everywhere at any time. What do you do with these people; what do you say? Do you arrest them? Tell them to go away? Ignore them as though they were not there? What do you do?

Jesus, our Lord, tells us that if we love Him, we will feed His sheep. The downtrodden, disinherited, disfranchised, and despondent persons must be ministered unto and the church, the body of Christ, must be at the forefront of seeing the stranger and taking them in.

How this is to be done can be found through searching the Scriptures with seeking heads and sensitive hearts.

Let us consider God's Word.

## Old Testament Perspective (References)

> You shall not wrong a stranger or oppress him, for you
> were strangers in the land of Egypt. You shall not afflict
> any widow or orphan. If you do afflict them and they cry
> out to me, I will surely hear their cry, and my wrath will
> burn; and I will kill you with the sword, and your wives
> shall become widows and your children fatherless (Ex.
> 22:21-24, RSV).

This first passage I have selected came from the Lord
to Israel, the covenant community. Based upon who
God is, what He had done, and what He required of His
people, the regulations and rules for their righteous
relationship with each other and with the stranger in
their presence were spelled out.

The Israelites were told specifically that they were
not to wrong or oppress the stranger. They must not
develop a religious exclusiveness that would falsely lead
them to believe that God's law is only applicable to
those in the covenant community; they must understand that their selection is to be a light to the nations.

The reason for defining their treatment of the stranger was because of their previous status of strangers in
the land of Egypt. A people who had known the alienation and hostility that came from being strangers in a
foreign land should have no problem identifying with
persons like themselves.

The warning was given in verse 23: if compassionate
love is not shown to the strangers, widows, and fatherless, the Lord said that His wrath would burn to such
a degree that they would be killed "and your wives
shall become widows and your children fatherless."

The church today is the covenant community of God,
we were once aliens and foreigners outside the com-
monwealth of Israel, and strangers from the covenant

of promises. We have a God-commanded mission to care for the stranger who is in our presence.

> When a stranger sojourns with you in your land, you shall not do him wrong. The stranger who sojourns with you shall be to you as the native among you, and you shall love him as yourself; for you were strangers in the land of Egypt. I am the Lord your God (Lev. 19:33-34, RSV).

From this passage, we can gather that there were two types of strangers or aliens who came among the Israelites. There was the transient stranger who would come among the people for a temporary time and then move on. The other was the resident alien who had more of a permanence with the people. The specific rules governing their treatment and behavior were spelled out. They were not to be mistreated and were to be loved as the Israelites loved themselves.

Many times when we read in the New Testament the words of Jesus saying to "love the Lord your God with all your heart, soul, and mind" and "love your neighbor as you love yourself," we think He is speaking something radically new. He is fulfilling what God's will has always been for His people.

From this passage, we view a clear biblical principle which gives a strategy for ministering to the strangers within our communities. We are not to wrong them either by verbally abusing them or physically neglecting to help them. We are to love them as we love ourselves. They are not to be related to as though they were the untouchables, or have some social plague that we must not come within fifty yards of them.

We are to love them with the approbate awareness of how God, through Jesus Christ, has shown His love for us.

What parent would see a son or daughter hungry, thirsty, dirty, and having no place to lay his/her head and not be moved to do all within their means to alleviate the situation? The Lord is saying in His Word that, just as you would help those within your family and those who belong to your church, so understand that the stranger is a part of your family; he or she is a part of God's pasture; they just need to be led and helped out of the muck and miry clay and led into green pastures.

> And if your brother becomes poor and cannot maintain himself with you, you shall maintain him; as a stranger and a sojourner, he shall live with you. Take no interest from him or increase, but fear your God; that your brother may live beside you. You shall not lend him your money at interest, nor give him your food for profit. I am the Lord your God who brought you forth out of the land of Egypt to give you the land of Canaan, and to be your God (Lev. 25:35-38, RSV).

This passage came as directions concerning the year of jubilee which came at the end of every forty-nine years. The land, all outstanding indebtness, slaves, and settlements were to be returned, redeemed, and reestablished.

If one of the Israelites had economic calamity, it was the responsibility of the family members and others in the community to look after him with compassionate care as though he were a stranger or a sojourner.

Help was to be given, but it was not to be done at the expense of the one needing the help. If food was needed, you were to give food and not put a price tag upon it. If money was needed, you were to give it, but not with interest attached. The whole purpose of all of this was to assist the person without taking advantage of their adverse situation.

The biblical principle is that when we see a stranger or sojourner in need, we are to help. We are not to do so for the purpose of gaining an advantage or seek to draw attention to the ministry. We are not providing so we can get the community award of the year for helping people.

> For the Lord your God is God of gods and Lord of lords; the great, the mighty, and the terrible God who is not partial and takes no bribe. He executes justice for the fatherless and the widow, and loves the sojourner, giving him food and clothing. Love the sojourner, therefore; for you were sojourners in the land of Egypt (Deut. 10:17-19, RSV).

Because of who God is and the covenant He has established with His people, the sojourner, alien, or stranger is to be cared for in the midst of the covenant community.

God is not partial in His lovingkindness or His tender mercy. He executes justice for the fatherless and the widow, and loves the stranger in giving him food and raiment. The Lord cannot be bribed into doing special favors or overlooking immorality or injustice. Christopher J. H. Wright in his book *An Eye for an Eye: The Place of Old Testament Ethics Today,* said that "failure to honour God in the material realm cannot be compensated for by religiosity in the spiritual realm."[1] This speaks to the heart of our faithful ministry and our failure to minister to the sojourner, the transient persons in our midst today. We somehow have lost our perspective (if for a certainty we ever had it) of what God commands of our doing justice and loving mercy.

Our ministry to the fatherless, widows, and to strangers is not to be done because we feel it would be nice to do something for those people. Our ministry to them must be done because we know it is what the sovereign God demands of us.

The Scripture text states that God gives them both food and raiment; something to eat, something to wear. The truth of God must always be translated into tangible acts. Love for the stranger, love for the fatherless, love for the widow is only an extension of our love for the Lord. It is our vertical connection with the Lord, sharing itself in a horizontal expression.

"No stranger had to spend the night in the street,/for my door was always open to the traveler" (Job 31:32, NIV). Job "defended" his case before the Lord and his "friends" that he had known and done the right thing concerning the stranger and the traveler.

With all of his abundance and wealth, Job had not overlooked his responsibility to share what he had with the stranger. The key point is not that this was the courteous or social thing to do; it was far greater than social etiquette, it had to do with "divine command." The strangers, the travelers were to be looked out for because the Lord was concerned about them.

The next time we see a stranger or a stranded traveler or someone needing help, let us not think in terms of "should I help?" God has already answered that question. Our question should be, "What is the best way I can help?"

> Is not this the kind of fasting I have chosen;
> to loose the chains of injustice
> and untie the cords of the yoke,
> to set the oppressed free
> and break every yoke?
> Is it not to share your food with the hungry
> and to provide the poor wandered with shelter;

when you see the naked, to clothe him,
and not to turn away from your own flesh and blood?
Isa. 58:6-7, NIV).

The Lord had much to say to His people through the prophets concerning their treatment and mistreatment of the strangers, the poor, and the defenseless. No religious ritual could replace their righteousness in their daily dealings with all men and women as precious in the sight of God.

The fast which the Lord called for is not just the refraining from eating or drinking; the Lord requires a fast of refraining from injustice, refusing to take a bribe, rejecting of the notion of impartial treatment.

Spiritual awareness must be shown in social action. God is the Provider and Sustainer and He gives the bread from heaven, but we, His people, have a responsibility to make the bread He gives available to all.

The Lord requires His people to do four things in our social actions: first share our food with the hungry; second, provide the poor wanderer with shelter; third, when we see the naked, clothe them; and fourth, do not turn away our own flesh and blood. Any church, any group, any individual who is compassionately conscious of their responsibility to the Lord to minister must be actively engaged in these kinds of ministries.

The Lord is not pleased with just our preaching, singing, and talking about love and justice; He is concerned that we declare it through our demonstration in our daily activity.

The last part of Isaiah 58 gives us the blessed promise of what the Lord will do for His people if they are obedient to Him.

The Lord tells them when they call, He will answer, "Your light will rise in the darkness, . . . The Lord will guide you always; he will satisfy your needs; . . . You will be like a well-watered garden,/like a spring whose waters never fail" (vv. 10-11, NIV).

Could it be that some of our prayers are not answered, we are in the dark concerning God's will and way, and we are constantly needing a revival to refresh our spiritual thirst, because we have neglected our responsibility to provide shelter for the wanderer, and food and clothing for the hungry and naked?

> If you really change your ways and your actions and deal with each other justly, if you do not oppress the alien [stranger], the fatherless or the widow and do not shed innocent blood in this place, and if you do not follow other gods to your own harm, then I will let you live in this place, in the land I gave your forefathers for ever and ever (Jer. 7:5-7, NIV).

The prophetic word is given concerning the judgment coming upon the people for their misuse of the strangers, fatherless, and widows. Other prophetic passages that should be considered are Jeremiah 22:3; Ezekiel 22:7, 29; Zechariah 7:10; Malachi 3:5. In each the theme is similar; do justly in your dealings with your neighbor and you will have righteousness with your God.

In the verses selected, we have the words of the Lord that came to Jeremiah as he preached his Temple sermon. It was a holy day of worship with the worshipers coming into the Temple of the Lord Much pomp and pageantry was in their processional. The incense was burning with a sweet smell, the music was melodious, the altars were prepared for the sacrifices, the priests were in position, the Torah was turned to the place of the day's Scripture reading, ushers, Levites, and all Temple personnel were in place. All was well except for one problem—no executing of righteousness in their daily activities.

What the Lord required of them and of us is to walk straight before we attempt to walk straight down His aisle in the Temple or church. What we do the other six days constitutes the worthiness or the worthlessness of our worship on Sunday. There can be no balancing of justice and mercy scales on Sunday for what we have failed to do on Monday.

People in the pew need to urgently understand this godly principle. Our worship of the Lord is only acceptable to the degree of our relationship in our dealings with our neighbor. No substitute or sacrifice can replace sincere service to minister to the needs of people, whether they be strangers, fatherless, or widows.

Why do we keep arguing over evangelism versus the social gospel? There is but one word and that is God's Word, and it encompasses all of life.

The next time you are on your way to church for worship services, ask yourself "Have the previous six days reflected my proper relationship with my Lord?" If you honestly cannot say yes, you need to do some amending before you get to the altar, change your course before you get to the choir stand, and reprioritize your plans before you get to the pulpit. If not, when you hear the call to worship, "The Lord is now in His holy temple, let all the earth keep silence before Him," you just may hear the Lord speak through the silence and say, "No, I am not."

In summarizing these selected Old Testament Scriptures, we see the same godly principle throughout. We are to treat the stranger as our neighbor, one of us. Our relationship to the stranger will be directly a determining factor in our relationship with our God. There can be no substitute for compassionate action. Our acceptance or unacceptance at the altar is based upon our awareness and move toward alleviating the hurt of those in the alley.

What God requires is for us "to do justly, and to love mercy, and to walk humbly with [our] God" (Mic. 6:8, KJV).

Let us now consider selected New Testament passages in coming to a better understanding of what Jesus meant when He said, "I was a stranger and you invited me in" (Matt. 25:35, NIV).

### New Testament Perspective

#### Luke 10:25-37

The parable of the good Samaritan provides an ideal paradigm or model for what authentic, genuine religion will do.

The context is a lawyer who asked Jesus what must he do to inherit eternal life. In His response, Jesus gave the love lesson of God and one's neighbor. To this, the lawyer wanted more explanation concerning who was his neighbor. Jesus gave him this story concerning a wounded man on the Jericho road.

Two reactions and one response were given to this wounded man. The priest saw human need but removed himself as far as possible away from it. He represents those persons who say they are followers of Jesus, but when Jesus cuts through the territory where the transients, strangers, street people, and skid row occupants dwell, they temporarily detour until Jesus gets back on the avenue or boulevard. They keep a safe gap between their brand of discipleship and desiring to deliver those who are in bondage.

The second reaction came from a Levite who saw

human need, moved toward it, but failed to aid. He saw the need, but kept his distance. The Levite represents those who say they are followers of the Lamb just as long as the Lamb leads and keeps them in green pastures and beside still waters. They have no identity or affinity with the downtrodden people of this world. They are dressed up for the Sunday worship; they have their assigned places in the church program and nothing, not even a wounded person beside their pathway, must prevent or hinder them from accomplishing their mission. Knowing that, these people will be pleased with their Scripture quotations and their solo for the special music on the order of service must not be altered.

The third person does not react, he responds. There are several "problems" with this man. First of all, he was a Samaritan. Certainly, because of his ethnic distinction he could not possibly be up to any good. Second, he went over to see the person and then moved compassionately to help. He surely must have been up to something. Third, he gave what he had, picked the individual up and placed him on his animal, took him to an inn, payed in advance for some of the expenses, and gave his credit card number to tally up any additional expenses.

What is the point in all of this? Jesus is teaching all of us that authentic religion shows itself in compassionate action toward every person whether male or female, black or white, poor or wealthy. We must not be too busy on our way to worship services that we fail to give service to those we encounter on the way.

Jesus said, "Inasmuch as you have done it unto the least of these my brethren, you have done it unto me" (Matt. 25:40, KJV). Love that has on overalls, work clothes, that is not afraid or ashamed of getting down where the hurt is, that's the acceptable service that the Lord demands of His people.

Just look around you. There are many wounded, forsaken, and attempted-to-be-forgotten folk along the Jericho road of life. You see them, I see them. What will be our next move? Will we react or will we respond?

"Now a bishop must be . . . hospitable" (1 Tim. 3:2, RSV). The word *hospitable* comes from the Latin word *hospitare*, meaning "to receive as a guest." It has the meaning of liberality, generosity, freely, shower down upon; open one's purse strings; give unsparingly, ungrudgingly.

This, states the Scripture text, is what a bishop (pastor —overseer) is to be and do. Given the sociopolitical environment of the first-century world, especially as it relates or, in many instances, did not relate in a positive way to those who were known as Christians, it can be understandable why a bishop would be instructed to exercise this characteristic.

The Greek word used for *hospitable* is the word *philoxenos* which literally means "loving strangers." The pastor-overseer of each local Christian community was to lovingly care for the strangers who would pass through their communities. Usually, the strangers would be other Christians who did not want to stay at roadside inns with pagan overtones, eating food which had been offered up to idols, and a usually debauched atmosphere.

This biblical principle is quite applicable for a ministry strategy for us today. Usually, one of the first places strangers, transients, aliens, or street people will seek refuge is on the steps of a church building. This is especially true if the church is located in a downtown, metropolitan area. Even if persons who are traveling the road experience any difficulty, they will seek out the church building or will ask the name of a local pastor to contact.

What should be the pastor-overseer response? According to our Scripture text, he is to love the strangers, not meet or greet them with contempt. He is to share whatever he has in a generous manner. Because of the high crime climate of our culture, he will have to exercise extreme caution in lodging persons in his home. He should provide such lodging by having already worked out an arrangement with a local motel or boarding house. Also, a local restaurant could assist in providing a meal.

A pastor-overseer must be hospitable.

"No widow may be put on the list of widows unless . . . she is well-known for her good deeds, such as . . . showing hospitality" (1 Tim. 5:9-10, NIV). It is interesting that one of the qualifiers for enrollment of the church's official widow list was whether the true widow had shown hospitality or not. She was expected to welcome strangers and do what she could for them. This would only be done as the widow understood that all that she had or ever hoped of getting came from the Lord who richly supplied her needs. She did not see herself so much as a server as being entrusted with the responsibility of caring for that which had been placed in her hands.

The pastor-overseer had a responsibility to the stranger and now we see that the widow had a responsibility to welcome strangers.

I wonder where the notion or idea got started that it is not the responsibility of the church community to care for those who are labeled "strangers" in our midst? Certainly Jesus never told us that; He said, "I was a stranger, and ye took me in" (Matt. 25:35, KJV). The Holy Spirit, in directing Paul to write his epistles, never told the pastor-overseer or the members of the Christian community not to minister to the needs of the stranger. I just wonder where and how this notion got started?

"Do not forget to entertain strangers; for by so doing, some people have entertained angels without knowing it" (Heb. 13:2, NIV). In this text, we have the writer's instruction and encouragement to entertain strangers because we are a Christian community called in love. Love will show itself in action to the others. There is also the possibility that in ministering to the stranger that you may be entertaining angels without knowing it.

If we believe, as I do, that the recipients of this letter were Jewish Christians, then the idea of receiving strangers would all the more be impressed upon them, since in this chapter we have surveyed selected passages in the Old Testament that showed Israel's responsibility to the stranger.

The idea of entertaining the strangers was not to be done to receive the approval of anyone; it was to be done as an expression that brotherly love was continuing. The authentic mark of a disciple, said Jesus, would be by the love they have for each other.

This text should help us see strangers from a different perspective; not as social rejects or public outcasts, but possible, just possibly, they could be angels. We will never know until we help them as best we can.

To entertain, then, is to hold the attention and the interest of the others. "Offer hospitality to one another without grumbling" (1 Pet. 4:9, NIV).

This thought of welcoming the stranger and loving them is further carried out in this verse. We are to offer hospitality, not in response to a regulation or as an expectant mode of behavior. Hospitality—loving service to render assistance—is to be done without grumbling.

There are many situations where assistance is given to the stranger or help is provided to the needy, but the person receiving the aid is clearly made to feel and know that it is not freely given.

If we give a cup of cold water in Jesus' name, we are to make sure that we give it as we have received, freely and abundantly.

> Dear friend, you are faithful in what you are doing for the brothers, even though they are strangers to you. They have told the church about your love. You will do well to send them on their way in a manner worthy of God. It was for the sake of the Name that they went out, receiving no help from the pagans. We ought, therefore, to show hospitality to such men so that we may work together for the truth (3 John 5-8, NIV).

This last collection of verses tells of the rejoicing report John had received from fellow traveling missionaries who were received warmly by Gaius. Gaius had shown the loving, welcoming reception to these brothers even though they were strangers to him. His gracious acts have been a source of warm witness to the church for all that he had done to encourage them by providing for them.

Several biblical principles are present to us in this section for developing ministry strategies.

*The first is faithfulness.* It was reported that Gaius was faithful in what he was doing for the brothers, even though they were strangers to him. His word and works were connected. His belief and behavior were consistent. His creed showed itself in his deeds.

*Second, good works are a witness of our discipleship.*

Because of what Gaius had done for these brethern, they have spoken well of his actions to the entire church. When one member is faithful to the Lord Jesus' commands, the whole church will benefit from it. If brother or sister John or Jane Doe does a good work and it is known what church they belong, the whole fellowship is looked upon in a good way. It is equally tragic, but true, if they are not kind or loving.

*Third, our ministry to others is a barometer of our ministry to our Lord.* We cannot isolate or separate what we do or do not do to the other person from what we think about and are willing to do for our Lord. Jesus said, "as we do to others, so we do to him."

*Fourth, we become co-laborers with the ministry and mission of Christ when we take His representatives, be they preachers, missionaries, the strangers, or the streetwalkers, and give them hospitality.* "I was a stranger, and ye took me in."

We have tried to show in this section of New Testament passages what our Lord meant when He said, "I was a stranger and you invited me in."

Let me share with you some ideas and information that will be helpful in ministering to the strangers in our presence.

### Guidelines for Future Ministries

1. Mission Houses
   To assist the church in her ministry to the strangers, transients, and street people, the church can purchase housing and make it available to shelter the homeless or those just passing through.
2. Low-Rent Subsidies
   The church can work out an agreement with suitable landlords to provide accommodations for per-

sons who are referred by the church and pay the rent on such dwelling.

3. Boarding Houses, Motels, and Hotels
   The church can have an arrangement with local hotels, motels, or boarding houses to provide temporary lodging or meals for those they are seeking to minister to.

4. Community Agencies
   The YMCA, YWCA, Salvation Army, college dormitories, and community centers all usually have temporary housing and sometimes meals are available. The church should be aware of these and have a relationship with them so that referrals can be made as the need presents itself.

5. Church Families
   Usually, in the church fellowship there will be persons who have an additional room or who would be willing to share their facilities for persons needing a temporary place to stay.

6. The Church Facility
   It is a sin that thousands of square feet of sanctuary, educational building, or Christian activities facilities remain unused for 80 percent of the time. Some of this space could be used to house strangers on a temporary basis. Many churches have modern-equipped kitchens that can easily prepare meals to feed several hundred, if not thousands at a time, and yet cannot, or do not, give two fish and five barley loaves to a hungry person.

7. Church Manors and Housing Units
   There is government money available to put up housing for the elderly, handicapped, and low-income persons. (At the time of this writing, the church where I serve as pastor, the Main Street Baptist Church, Lexington, Kentucky, just re-

ceived $2.1 million grant from the Department of Housing and Urban Development for such a project.) It can be done, if your motive is to glorify the Lord by doing it for the least of these.

# 4
# Feeding the Naked

*"I was naked and you clothed me" (Matt. 25:36, RSV).*

In this chapter, we will look at selected passages from both the Old and New Testaments to try to understand better what the divine mandates are concerning clothing the naked.

From our biblical survey, we will discover principles from which we can develop ministry strategies to not only endorse what Jesus is saying to us, but once it is endorsed, to execute it through application.

What did Jesus mean when He said, "I was naked and you clothed me?"

As we begin our study, let us consider briefly some of the basic clothes items that would have been worn during the time of Jesus.

### The Inner Garment—Tunic or Shirt

The tunic (inappropriately translated "coat") was a shirt which was worn next to the skin. It was made of leather, haircloth, wool, linen, or in modern times, usually of cotton. The simplest form was without sleeves and reached to the knees or sometimes to the ankles. The well-to-do wore it with sleeves and extending to the ankles.[1]

Among the lower classes, the tunic was often the only article worn in warm weather. Personnel of higher rank might wear the tunic alone inside the house, but would not wear it without the outer garment outside, or when they were to receive a caller. In the Bible, the term "naked" is used of men clad only with their tunic (cf. Isa. 20:2-4; Mic. 1:8; John 21:7). To be dressed in such a scanty manner was thought of as "nakedness."[2]

As a rule, the Jews of Christ's day had at least a change of apparel. A man would be considered poor to have only one garment.[3]

### The Girdle

If the tunic was ungirded, it would interfere with a person's ability to walk freely; and so a girdle was always worn when leaving home for any kind of a journey (see 2 Kings 4:29; Acts 12:8). There were, and are today, two kinds of girdles. One, a common variety, is of leather, usually six inches wide and furnished with clasps. This was the kind of girdle worn by Elijah (2 Kings 1:8), and by John the Baptist (Matt. 3:4). The other, a more valuable variety, is of linen (see Jer. 13:1), or sometimes of silk or embroidered material. It is generally a handbreadth wide. The girdle also served as a pouch in which to keep money (2 Sam. 18:11) and other things that might be needed (Mark 6:8). The girdle was used to fasten a man's sword to his body (1 Sam. 25:13). Thus, the girdle was a very useful part of a man's clothing.[4]

### The Outer Garment—Mantle

The outer garment, which the Palestinian villager wears, is a large cloak which would serve the purpose of a Westerner's overcoat. It is made of wool or goat's hair and sometimes of cotton. It serves as a shelter from the wind and rain, and as a blanket at night.[5]

The law of Moses contained an explicit commandment regarding this outer garment. This is the way the law reads:

> If thou at all take thy neighbor's raiment to pledge, thou shalt deliver it unto him by that the sun goeth down. For that is his covering only; it is his raiment for his skin: wherein shall he sleep? And it shall come to pass, when he crieth unto me, that I will hear; for I am gracious (Ex. 22:26-27, KJV).

It was because this outer garment was a man's covering by night that the law did not allow anyone to take it as a pledge or security, for this would deprive him of the means of keeping warm while sleeping. Being closely woven, it is warm, and if he sleeps out of doors, this covering is even waterproof.[6]

Because of the fullness of the mantle, it served as a means of carrying various things. The lap was often filled with grain or fruit. Ruth could put six measures of barley into her mantle (Ruth 3:15). It could be used as a saddlecloth and even as a carpet to welcome great men.[7]

### Headdress

In public, the Jews always wore a turban; for at certain seasons of the year it is dangerous in Palestine to expose one's head to the rays of the sun. This turban was of thick material and passed several times around the head. It was somewhat like our handkerchief and was made of linen, or recently of cotton.[8]

### Sandals

The shoes, as worn by the majority in New Testament times, were, no doubt, what we would call sandals. They consisted of a sole of wood or leather, which was fastened to the foot by leather thongs.[9]

From this brief survey of the clothing items worn during Jesus' day, we can glean some important insights concerning what Jesus meant when He said, "I was naked and you clothed Me."

For a person to have only a tunic or undergarment was to be considered naked. He would have only the bare necessity to cover his physical nakedness.

Not to have the mantle or cloak, as it is sometimes called, would mean that one was deprived of a most essential piece of clothing. As has been stated, fruit and grain could be carried in the mantle. Even a small lamb could be placed there. It was used for a protective covering at night to keep one both warm and dry. Not to have this piece of clothing would mean you would be totally exposed to the elements and possibly not have the basic essentials of food to sustain yourself on your journey.

The turban was used as a head covering and as a protection from the dangerous sun rays. Not to have a head covering could prevent one from entering the Temple and also present a health hazard with possible heat stroke.

The girdle held everything in place, being used as a pouch to carry money, to fasten the sword to a man's body, and also as a pouch to carry whatever would be of value. For a person not to have a girdle would be considered "naked" because they would have no money on them, nor have anything to protect themselves.

The sandals were necessary as one moved over the rocky terrain. Not to have sandals or shoes was a sign of a servant or slave. Thus, to be without sandals, you were considered "naked"; you were totally at the command and care of your master if you were a slave or servant.

In all of these briefly cited examples, we can see that
Jesus was saying, when you saw Me (and, in the broaden
sense, when you saw anyone) without these basic necessities, you either gave them to Me (or them) or you did
not. The true level of your love for Me, says Jesus, is the
determined degree you moved to cover My nakedness.

Let us look at selected biblical passages, scanning
both the Old and New Testaments, to hear our Lord
speak to us through His word concerning those who are
naked and what our ministry should be to them.

### Old Testament Perspective

"And the man and his wife were both naked, and
were not ashamed" (Gen. 2:25, RSV). This first reference in the Bible to nakedness is used to show that
nakedness, in the beginning, was not the deprived or
destitute state which it now is. The man and his wife
were not ashamed of their gender or genitals. There
was no sin that had separated them or caused them to
be in a rebellious state with their Creator.

The goodness and graciousness of God had adequately clothed them in righteousness and purity. The one
did not see the other as separate or hostile, but rather
they saw each other as mutual.

When, by the grace of God, we are returned to the
ideal state of perfect harmony with God and with each
other, we will see all people as our mutual brothers or
sisters; there will be no destitution or depravity and,
thusly, no need to be ashamed. Until that time, we must
work to clothe the nakedness of this world with righteousness, justice, and truth.

> The the eyes of both were opened, and they knew that
> they were naked; and they sewed fig leaves together
> and made themselves aprons (Gen. 3:7, RSV).

What had happened? One minute they were naked and no shame, the next they were naked and attempting to cover themselves.

The open, honest, whole relationship that man and woman had with God the Creator was now one of hiding from His presence. They attempted to do something about their nakedness that, up to that point, had not even been an issue.

Man and woman, in their futile attempts, tried to alleviate what God had made them to be—open and free with Him and with each other. The quest for the other made man and woman different and estranged from each other.

The sewing of fig leaves was a human attempt to remove or blot out our nakedness before the open and watchful eyes of God. Human fig leaves today are made out of consumerism, materialism, and consumption. We simply do not want to own up to the reality that separates us from God because we are naked and undone.

In many churches, we attempt to sew fig leaves made of stained glass to shut out the naked reality of brothers and sisters who are deprived of the necessities of life. We sew fig leaves of mission and benevolent offerings so that we can give a few coins to keep the naked from approaching our doorsteps. We even give plaques and awards to those who will go in our place to carry the fig leaf material so our fur-colored eyes do not have to glance upon their naked bodies.

I hear Jesus speaking to me—do you hear Him speaking to you? "Do you love Me?"; "Yes, Lord." "Then feed (clothe) My sheep."

"Bring Aaron and his sons to the entrance to the Tent of Meeting and wash them with water. Then dress

Aaron in the sacred garments, annoint him and conse-
crate him so he may serve me as priest. Bring his sons
and dress them in tunics. Anoint them just as you
anointed their father, so they may serve me as priests.
Their anointing will be to a priesthood that will contin-
ue for all generations to come." Moses did everything
just as the Lord commanded him (Ex. 40:12-16, NIV).

This selection has been chosen to depict the unique
clothing items that the priests of God were to wear.
Aaron and his sons had been set apart for a special
ministry of serving as priests among the people. They
were to be God's representatives, intercessors, and
mediators. The purpose of their special garments were
not so they could be seen, but rather that they might
serve the people.

We who are in the body of Christ are a royal priesthood uniquely clothed in righteousness, grace, and humility. Our "clothing" is not to make us spectacles to be
gazed at but to be servants to offer the free gift of God's
grace.

If we seriously seek ways to clothe the naked, caring
for those who are destitute among us, we must be sure
we are properly clothed ourselves. Our garments, as
Aaron's garments, must be a daily reminder to all of
God's people that He is among His people and we make
His presence known by the service we offer.

The priesthood of Aaron and our priesthood is not to
be of the seasonal type—you know—giving out baskets
of goodies at Thanksgiving or Christmastime. Our
priesthood is to be perpetually, forever present.

There is a key principle in verse 16. "Moses did everything just as the Lord commanded him." It was not
only that Moses knew what to do that was acceptable,
it was the fact that he knew what to do and did it. We
see many naked people and know we could give them

a piece of clothing, assist them in some small or even
great way, but we alibi and attempt to rationalize and
justify our lack of ministry involvement. No, my brothers and sisters, knowing is not enough; it takes both
knowing and doing to be acceptable in God's sight.

> At this, Job got up and tore his robe and shaved his head.
> Then he fell to the ground in worship and said:
> "Naked I came from my mother's womb,
> and naked I will depart.
> The Lord gave and the Lord has taken away;
> may the name of the Lord be praised."
> In all this, Job did not sin by charging God with wrong-
> doing (Job 1:20-22, NIV).

Tragedy had infiltrated Job's tranquility, and trouble
was about to teach him some awesome lessons. The
summation of events from where Job sat were; I came
into the world naked and will depart the world the
same way. I did not get anything, the Lord gave; it was
His to give and it is certainly His to take away.

The ministry principle for us to see is to have the
freedom to release what we have been given, by giving
it back to the Giver.

This is quite contrary to our consumer-oriented,
possessive-minded society. We must see all things as a
gift from God and, thus, to be used as an expression of
the graciousness of God to the other. As long as we
erroneously conclude that what we have is ours, we will
forever be in a state of anxiety, trying to hold on to it,
protect it, and keep it. Once we understand that we are
the possessors with a temporary contract to use what
we have, knowing we will have to give an account of
what we have done or have not done, we are in a position to help the helpless, feed the hungry, and clothe
the naked. You would have to agree that many people

have the means to help, but they do not have the mind to do so.

Naked I came and naked I will depart; whatever I accummulate between my coming and my departing, let me use it wisely and generously.

> You demanded security from your brothers for no reason;
> you stripped men of their clothing, leaving them naked.
> You gave no water to the weary,
> and you withheld food from the hungry,
> though you were a powerful man, owning land (Job 22:6-8, NIV).

These words fell from the lips of Eliphaz, the "friend" of Job. They were Eliphaz's futile attempt to explain Job's present predicament.

The reason Eliphaz gave for all the calamity and chaotic conflicts that had happened in Job's life was because his wickedness was great and his iniquities were infinite. None of this was true, of course, but it was Eliphaz's way of trying to make sense out of chaos.

Let us clearly consider the charges and, for reflective purposes, assume that they are true.

First—"You demand security from your brothers for no reason; you stripped men of their clothing, leaving them naked." The idea here is that the important piece of clothing called the mantle, or cloak, could be used as a security deposit or down payment for the purchase of things. It also could be given as a good faith bond, expressing the trustworthiness of the borrower. As stated earlier, this piece of clothing was quite important because of many uses; namely, as a covering of protection from the elements, a blanket at night, a container for food items, and as a covering like a saddle for riding upon animals. The law explicitly made it clear that at

sunset you were to return it to your neighbor. (See Ex.
22:26-27.) Not to give it back would leave one naked,
both in protection and provisions.

The second charge Eliphaz made against Job was that
he had not given water to the weary nor bread to the
hungry even "though you were a powerful man, owning land." To not do this would constitute breaking the
law by not caring for one's neighbor as oneself. Job
would be deserving of his painful lot because he had the
means to help but refused to help. Certainly for Job,
none of these charges were correct; for he had cared for
the downtrodden.

The biblical principle for us to see in all of this is that
God's wrath and judgment does come upon individuals,
groups, businesses, and even churches who do such
things. When we have the means to help, we must also
have the mind and the method to help. To take advantage of the destitute is to literally slap God in His face.
That is why Jesus said, "When you have or have not
done it unto the least of these, you have or have not
done it unto Me."

> Is it not to share your food with the hungry
> and to provide the poor wanderer with shelter—
> when you see the naked, to clothe him,
> and not to turn away from your own flesh and blood?
> (Isa. 58:7, NIV).

This passage comes from an oracle given by Isaiah
during the post-Exilic period. The people had sought
the Lord by being careful to observe the worship tradition and by being obedient to the teaching of the law
as they understood it. They had sought the Lord daily
and had even gone to the point of fasting to empty
themselves that they might be filled with the Lord's
presence. None of this had worked and the Lord spoke

through Isaiah, telling the people that the true fast which the Lord requires is not the doing-without type, but rather doing by helping the wanderer, the naked, the destitute, those who are ill-treated, righting the wrongs of injustice, and feeding the hungry.

What a message for us! Religious formality and ritual observances are never acceptable to the Lord by themselves. What the Lord requires is that we execute justice and compassionate care for the needy who are among us. Not fasting, but feeding; not observance, but obedience—this is what the Lord requires.

There are far too many good, religious people who would spend enormous amounts of money on choir robes, usher uniforms, special-day outfits to do "service" at the temple, but would be hesitant or even refuse to give more than fifty cents to help clothe the naked. They would purchase banquet tickets and get front-row, reserved seating at a religious or social event, but would refuse to bring one canned item to place in a food basket for the hungry.

The Lord says that religious acts will never suffice for righteous actions in doing justly and loving mercy. Fasting is acceptable; just make sure that the food you refrain from eating finds a resting place in the mouths and stomachs of the hungry. Put on the choir robe; just make sure you also put some shirts and socks on the backs and feet of the naked. If you do this, then you will have something to shout about.

From this brief sketch of Old Testament passages, we can see that the garment that is acceptable to the Lord is goodness which shows itself in gracious acts. The tunic must be truth, the mantle—mercy, the headdress —holiness, the girdle—grace, and the sandals must be sincere, seeking always to help the destitute.

Let us turn our attention now to the New Testament

to get a further perspective on what Jesus meant when
He said, "I was naked and you clothed Me."

## New Testament Perspective

> And she brought forth her firstborn son, and wrapped
> him in swaddling clothes, and laid him in a manger;
> because there was no room for them in the inn (Luke
> 2:7, KJV).

I believe the ideal place to start our study of this
clothes business is to see what Jesus had to wear at His
birth. The Scripture states that Mary wrapped Him in
swaddling clothes. These were strips of cloth like band-
ages, wrapped around young infants to keep their limbs
straight (see Ezek. 16:4). That Jesus was laid in a man-
ger, because there was no room for them in the inn,
adds to the unacceptable reception Jesus received
when He came into the world.

Jesus' wardrobe was quite limited. In fact, the only
mention of His garments is when Jesus was crucified,
and then the soldiers "took His garments and made
four parts." To not destroy his tunic or undergarment,
because it was one piece woven without seams, they
cast lots to see who would get it (see John 19:23-24).
Thus, we have the beginning and the ending of Jesus'
clothing. Swaddling clothes at the beginning and
stripped of His seamless tunic at the end. Could this add
some light to what Jesus said, "[When you saw me]
naked, and ye clothed me not"? (KJV).

> And why do you worry about clothes? See how the lilies
> of the field grow. They do not labor or spin. Yet, I tell
> you that not even Solomon, in all his splendor, was
> dressed like one of these. If that is how God clothes the
> grass of the field, which is here today and tomorrow is

thrown into the fire, will he not much more clothe you, O you of little faith? (Matt. 6:28-30, NIV).

The next time we hear Jesus addressing Himself to this clothes issue, He asked a probing and penetrating question, "And why do you worry about clothes?" Several answers come to my mind quickly. Because I am modest and shy and do not want to expose my naked body. Because I am style conscious, I want to wear the acceptable thing. Because I believe my first impression is the lasting impression. My status and position are directly related to what I wear. Because I want to inform and impress people with my financial clout, thus, I wear only designer and one-of-a-kind outfits. The list could go on and on, but I hope your answer fits somewhere in there; if not, fill in the gap.

The question comes back to confront us—Why do you worry about clothes?

The answer is given by Jesus. He says the reason we worry about our clothes is because we have not considered the lilies of the field. What do lilies have to do with labels, and the field with fashion? Everything. Consider the Source. Since God the Father dresses the barren fields, you can trust Him to dress you.

When you see a naked person, you do not just tell them to trust God to clothe them without providing the means of that trust. You tell them to trust God and then you demonstrate that trust by giving them something to wear. God is the Source of what they need and of what you have to offer. Worry slanders the promises of God. When you worry about what you are going to wear or if you are going to have anything to wear, you are really saying, "Can I trust God to do what He has promised that He would do?"

Faith is the other key to unlock our understanding.

Faith says: God can, God will and God cares. When we see the naked, the destitute, those without, we must never pretend the situation is not as we see it. We must move on an affirmation that, in spite of the situation, God is able to redeem it. God can provide, He will provide, and He cares enough to provide. The question on our agendas should be, What part does the Lord want us to play in His redeeming process? How this works is quite simple. If we see someone who is naked and we have spring, summer, fall, and winter clothing, clothing in storage, and clothes for special events put away, we cannot honestly ask the Lord to provide for the naked person. We have to take what the Lord has already given and give to the person as the Lord has given to us. When you consider the Source of all things, you can consider all persons as God's creatures who are of infinite worth to Him.

> The disciples went and did as Jesus had instructed them. They brought the donkey and the colt, placed their cloaks on them, and Jesus sat on them. A very large crowd spread their cloaks on the road, while others cut branches from the trees and spread them on the road (Matt. 21:6-8, NIV).

The scene is the royal entry of Jesus in Jerusalem. He did not come into Jerusalem as the earthly kings did with their long processional of cabinet and staff, with military aides, captors from the war with booty. Jesus came in a low and meek manner. It was clearly a demonstration that His Kingdom is not of this world.

The disciples placed their cloaks, which we have described in the first part of this chapter as being the outer garment and being of considerable use and worth, upon the animal as Jesus mounted up. As Jesus approached the city and began his entry, a large crowd spread their cloaks on the road, while others cut the branches from palm trees and also spread them on the road.

The equivalent of taking off your cloak and placing it in the road would be for us to take off our overcoat (our good overcoat, I might add) and place it on the asphalt street while an important person passed by. This is sometimes called giving the red carpet treatment.

The text speaks to us at the point of taking off our cloak, our overcoat, our expensive and necessary piece of clothing, and placing it at the disposal of Jesus. Jesus is still riding into every city, town, and village. And we use what we have in placing it not on the backs of donkeys, but on the backs of the naked and destitute among us.

They took their cloaks and placed them in the street. We need to take our cloaks and clothe somebody. Size up the fatherless, the widow, the refugee, the unemployed, the mentally handicapped, the street people; knowing that when we do, we are doing unto Jesus our Lord and Savior.

"When they had crucified him, they divided up his clothes by casting lots" (Matt. 27:35, NIV). It was customary that the one being crucified would be stripped of his clothing. The clothes would become the property of the executioners. In Jesus' case, the soldiers did not want to tear the seamless robe which Jesus had—destroying its worth. So they cast lots to see who would get it.

There Jesus was, the one who had come to clothe the believer in righteousness and mercy, hung naked upon a rugged cross. He had come to lift men and women out of their bondage and now His place of residence was on a hill called Golgatha.

They took our Lord's clothing that day. They left

Him naked and exposed. You ask, How can we get the clothes back on Him? Jesus gives the answer, "I was naked and you clothed Me." Whenever you see a person naked and destitute, a person who has received injustice, persons wounded because of their crucifixions in this life, and you go to serve them in the name of Jesus, you are putting His clothes back on Him.

Simply standing at the foot of the cross and crying will not do it. Standing with a compassionate heart in the doorway of a home will begin to wipe the tears out of both Jesus' eyes and yours.

> As he taught, Jesus said, "Watch out for the teachers of the law. They like to walk around in flowing robes and be greeted in the marketplaces, and have the most important seats in the synagogues and the places of honor at banquets. They devour widows' houses and, for a show, make lengthy prayers. Such men will be punished most severely" (Mark 12:38-40, NIV).

In this selection of Scripture, Jesus teaches about scribes, suits, salutations, special seating, schemes, and the saying of prayers. That which is of particular interest to us is the long flowing robes the scribes wore, called tallith, which was supposed to signify piety and scholarship. At the bottom of the robes on the four corners were the fringes which were tassels of the outer garment (see Num. 15:37-41). These fringes were to be a constant reminder to the children of Israel of their covenant commitment in keeping the commandments of their Lord.

Jesus condemns the scribes, not for the wearing of these garments, but for their motive and method of wearing them. They went to the extent of making them extremely long so as to be noticeable. They were more concerned about drawing the people's attention to

themselves as interpreters of the law rather than actually keeping the law.

Our clothing also gives us away as to our motive for
ministry. Pulpit garments, choir robes, ushers' uniforms, nursery smocks, kitchen aprons, Sunday School
badges, and pins all serve their unique purpose of identifying and distinguishing us as to our ministries, but
none of these things must become the barrier prevent-
ing us from "clothing the naked." Great amounts of
money will be freely spent to decorate the sanctuary,
keep the piano and organ tuned, the floors carpeted
and waxed, but when it comes time to drape a dress
over a destitute person, a committee has to be organized, a board has to meet, a congregation has to vote.

When we do this, Jesus says anew and afresh,
"Beware of the scribes" (KJV). Let us show the greater
zeal in clothing the naked than we do in color-coordina-
tion consciousness, making sure the carpet and ceiling
colors do not clash.

"A young man, wearing nothing but a linen garment,
was following Jesus. When they seized him, he fled
naked, leaving his garment behind" (Mark 14:51-52,
NIV).

The context of this is the arrest of Jesus in the garden
of Gethsemane. When the soldiers came and took Jesus,
all fled and forsook Him.

A certain young man, having only a linen garment
around him, followed Jesus. Who he was is left to speculation. I believe that his personal identity is not the
point of the Holy Spirit directing the writer to include
this in the Gospel. The biblical principle is what is significant.

When we choose to follow Jesus, there is a risk factor
always present. The risk of being misunderstood, the
risk of being misused, the risk of being forsaken by

others. There also is the biblical principle of sacrifical service when we seek Jesus. This young man was captured, but managed to escape only after he left his garment behind.

When we hear Jesus' call to clothe the naked, He is saying, "Follow Me, and be fully aware of the risk factor." There will be the risk that when you go to clothe the naked, the "nice" people will misunderstand you. Your motives will be questioned, and your method will be doubted.

There is also the possibility that you will have to engage in sacrificial service. Going to the naked does not give you a guarantee that they will take only what you offer them; they may take your garment from you. If you approach a person with no suit, in your three-piece suit and offer them a pair of socks, they may take the socks and want your suit, shirt, and matching accessories.

The assurance in all of this is the words of Jesus— "Inasmuch as ye have done it unto the least of these my brethren, ye have done it unto me" (Matt. 25:40, KJV).

"So he [Jesus] got up from the meal, took off his outer clothing, and wrapped a towel around his waist" (John 13:4, NIV). Jesus, the host of this meal with His disciples in an upper room in Jerusalem, did the host thing. It was customary for the host to have a servant and most commonly a slave wash the feet of his guests. Jesus performed the service of the servant Himself. He took off the outer clothing, which would be the cloak, laid it aside, took a towel and girded Himself, which meant to pull up or make oneself accessible for service. Jesus washed the disciples' feet and, in doing so, taught them the greatest lesson in humble service.

The biblical principle for our ministry strategy in

clothing the naked can be summed up with: get up, pull off, put on, and serve.

Let us look at the passage once again. Jesus got up from the meal. Jesus was eating and the disciples were eating; but in order to "feed them," He got up from the meal. If we are going to minister in Jesus' name, we have to get up from our tables of overabundance and go over and apply some love, justice, and mercy.

Jesus pulled off His outer garment. This made it easier for Him to serve. We must pull off pride, self-righteousness, importance, and stand ready to be of service.

Jesus put on the towel—not a robe, a crown, or a uniform of distinction, but a towel. We must put on humility, meekness, an attitude of willingness to be used and usable by the Lord.

Jesus served. All of the getting up, pulling off, and putting on was for the purpose of serving. Jesus said, "If you love Me, feed (clothe) My sheep." You do so by getting up, pulling off, putting on, and serving.

> We are fools for Christ, but you are so wise in Christ! We are weak, but you are strong! You are honored, we are dishonored! To this very hour we go hungry and thirsty; we are in rags, we are brutally treated, we are homeless (1 Cor. 4:10-11, NIV).

Paul wrote to refute the Corinthians for their boasting in their prominence, their position, and place of superiority. He had to remind them that whoever they were, and whatever they may have had, it came from the Lord. In contrast to that feeling of sufficiency and adequately being provided for, Paul said that he and the other apostles were fools for Christ. They were hungry, thirsty, poorly clothed, brutally treated, and they were homeless.

What a radically different view from what many on

the American religious scene have concerning those who do the Lord's work—radio, television, and the mass media which saturates us with success and positive living for Jesus' sake that we hear over and over again. They say that if you just believe, you will have no more burdens, no more bills, and no more bunions; just blessings, blessings, blessings!

Paul believed in Jesus; in fact, he had experienced Him on the Damascus road. He had faith, he had trusted Him, was obedient, walked by faith, lived in hope, was waiting patiently for the Lord's return and, yet, Paul wrote of himself and his fellow apostles. They went hungry, thirsty, were poorly clothed, brutally treated, and homeless.

Those who had been clothed in righteousness and suited according to grace were poorly clothed physically. The biblical principle for us is that our faith in Jesus does not remove us from the real world with all of its difficulties and dreadful moments. Neither does the fact that if we are lacking in total sufficiency and supply ourselves, we are relieved and released of our responsibility to minister according to our Lord's plan.

Paul did not say, "Look, I am without adequate food, clothing, and shelter myself; when I get myself together, then I will be in a position to help others." There are far too many good-intentioned people waiting to get themselves together first and then they are going to turn the world upside down—so they falsely believe.

We must minister with the means that we have, always being mindful that if we have only one three-piece suit, we may need to break it down into three one-piece suits. That is if we really love the Lord.

Nothing in all creation is hidden from God's sight. Everything is uncovered and laid bare before the eyes of him to whom we must give account (Heb. 4:13, NIV).

This passage has been selected because it speaks specifically about our seriousness and sincerity in doing the Lord's work. The previous verse talks about the word of God being able to penetrate our deepest motives and intentions. We must be constantly on the alert that when we are doing the Lord's work in our context of clothing the naked, that we are doing so because of our love and loyalty to our Lord.

A person can do good deeds with the wrong motives. Nothing in all creation is hidden from God's sight. Not only does God know about the fruit, He knows about the leaves, branches, roots, stems, seeds, and soil. We could provide clothing to the other and still be found naked ourselves. Let us be conscious and cautious in how we minister; paying particular attention to why we minister, realizing we are going to have to give an account for both what we do and do not do.

> What good is it, my brothers, if a man claims to have faith but has no deeds? Can such faith save him? Suppose a brother or sister is without clothes and daily food. If one of you says to him, "Go, I wish you well; keep warm and well fed," but does nothing about his physical needs, what good is it? In the same way, faith, by itself, if it is not accompanied by action, is dead (Jas. 2:14-17, NIV).

A regenerative faith will show itself in regenerated actions. The believers' behavior will show itself in the deeds that are done. Faith that is rooted in the living God will produce fruit.

The writer was using hyperbole or overstatement to make the reality of rejecting the request of a needed person come to life for the person who wants to claim faith without the appropriate action. The preached word must become the practiced word; the sung word must become the serving word. Our prayers must never be substitutes for our refusal to relieve the downtrodden.

A hungry, thirsty, naked, and homeless individual does not need to just be remembered in prayer, he or she needs to be remembered at the meal, clothing, or house-building time, and then take what you can to help them.

Too many benevolent groups, mission committees, relief boards, and agencies have met, eating banquet meals, feasting on the fat of the land while they are praying, planning, and plotting a strategy to feed the hungry. Persons show up at these meetings and have to either get a coat check number or place their minks and furs under protective custody while they discuss the naked and shelterless among them.

It is really quite simple to help, if you are serious about helping. Do. Give.

> To the angel of the church in Laodicea, write: These are the words of the Amen, the faithful, and true witness, the ruler of God's creation. You say, "I am rich; I have acquired wealth and do not need a thing." But you do not realize that you are wretched, pitiful, poor, blind, and naked. I counsel you to buy from me gold refined in the fire, so you can become rich; and white clothes to wear, so you can cover your shameful nakedness; and salve to put on your eyes, so you can see (Rev. 3:14,17-18, NIV).

A church can be naked. We see the prime example of this in the church at Laodicea. Laodicea was known for its wealth and resulting independence, for its medical school with ointments for the eyes and ears, and its thriving clothing industry; notably, black wool. These conditions had crept into the church. The Laodicean Christians had concluded that since they were financially wealthy, and had what was needed to maintain themselves year after year, they were complete. The witness against them is that just where they thought they were "hot," they were "lukewarm," ready to be spit out.

This Laodicean church tragically represents many churches in America. We measure our religious success by bricks, budgets, and baptisms. Is it not amazing that a church building that once could seat one hundred, adds a few feet of space to where they now can seat one hundred twenty-five, and all of a sudden it becomes the Greater _____ Church? The financial balance sheet can show that five hundred members gave, on the average, five dollars more for the entire year and we can falsely conclude we are doing fine—because the budget was met. Or in like manner, we baptized six last year and this year we baptized eight—boy, are we growing! I hope you get the picture.

Jesus Christ, the Head of the church at Laodicea and the Head of all churches that minister in His name, says to all, "You are poor if you have not given your riches to feed the hungry, water the thirsty, clothe the naked, visit the sick, go to those in prison, shelter the stranger. You are blind if you cannot see that inasmuch as you have done it unto the least of these My brethren, you have done it unto Me."

Is the church where you belong and attend a Laodicean church, or a Jesus' church?

After this, I looked and there before me was a great multitude that no one could count, from every nation, tribe, people, and language, standing before the throne and in front of the Lamb. They were wearing white robes and were holding palm branches in their hands (Rev. 7:9, NIV).

This chapter would not be complete without closing on the positive note of affirmation that is coming the day when persons of various ethnic and cultural differences, those who have washed their robes in the blood of the Lamb assemble before His throne.

Those who will be wearing these white robes are those who have salvation and victory. They will receive these robes because in this life they were willing to pull off what they had to put it on someone else. They were willing to serve even at the cost of sacrifice and, in some cases, physical death. They are the one who became naked that others might be clothed.

There is the promise of paramount provision for those who love the Lord by serving Him in this life. Many are naked now and some are clothed in temporary garments, but there is coming a day when all we who love the Lord will stand before His throne clothed with white robes and palms in our hands. "Do you love Me?" Yes, Lord, you know I do. "[Then] feed [clothe] My sheep."

### Guidelines for Future Ministries

1. Church Clothes Closets

A designated person and location can be assigned to receive clothes items donated by members who will. These items should be clean and in good condition. These items can be distributed as the requests are made. When there are no requests and there is an accumulation of goods, they can be given to community agencies.

2. Church Family Exchange Program

On a given day, church members can bring clothing items and exchange with other members. This works well, especially with children's clothes. Also, the surplus clothes could be given to those in the community who have nothing to exchange.

3. Co-op Buying

The church, as a nonprofit organization, can sometimes purchase clothes items in bulk at a wholesale price and pass the savings on to members in both the church and the community.

4. Church Clusters

Churches in an area can come together and unite their resources and efforts to meet the needs of the naked and destitute in a given neighborhood. If the law of love and unity prevails, this could be a citywide project.

5. Clothes Showers

You have heard of baby showers; why not have an adult shower? Clothes items could be brought to help a family or an individual. Clothing of deceased persons are often discarded quickly and recklessly. Why not organize a committee to take care of this matter, seeing that those in need receive assistance?

6. Church Community Agencies

The local church can and should work with other agencies in the community that seek to help clothe the naked. Keeping abreast of fires, tornadoes, and other emergencies in the community, take advantage of a blessed opportunity to minister to someone in Jesus' name.

7. Teaching of Clothes Stewardship

Clothes ranks in about the top seven or eight items that the average American family spends their income on. Practicing wise clothes purchasing, taking advantage of when a sale is really a sale, and learning how to coordinate and correlate clothes, could all help on the monthly expense of such items. Becoming need conscious rather than want or style conscious could also help with expenditures for clothes—leaving more to share with someone else.

# 5
# Feeding the Sick

*"I was sick, and ye visited me" (Matt. 25:36, KJV).*

Jesus said, "I was sick and you visited Me." The word for sick is *astheneō* which means "to be feeble, weak, without strength." I am in bondage because of my infirmities. My illness has caused me to fall down both with myself and with others.

Jesus said, "You visited Me." The word for visit is *episkeptomai* which primarily means "to inspect, to look upon, care for, exercise oversight."

Jesus is saying to you and me, "When I was feeble, weak and without strength, you came and visited or inspected Me. You came to care for Me and exercise oversight over Me."

The questions come back from the corridors of the judgment hall—When did we see You sick or without strength? When did we not come to care for You and to exercise oversight over You? Jesus replies, "Inasmuch as you did not do it unto the least of these you did not do it unto Me."

This author has heard for too long and too often the expression of petitions made in prayers for the sick, "Lord, go by the hospitals, visit in every sick room, cool scorching fevers, and ease racking pain."

If my interpretation of what Jesus our Lord is saying to us in this passage is correct, *we* have the responsibility to go to those who are feeble and without strength and to exercise caring oversight over them.

## What Does It Mean to Feed the Sick?

Let us get a biblical overview by looking at selected Old Testament passages and New Testament passages for the Scriptural principles from which we can develop ministry strategies.

### Biblical Perspectives: Old Testament

The concept that healing is of divine origin was deeply noted in all Hebrew thought, even becoming a part of the daily ritual. The effect of the monotheistic concept in Israel was of prime importance as the function of healing was ascribed solely to God. The one God was the Source of all disease and all health, either directly or indirectly. Basic to the idea of God as Healer was the concept of God's conservation of nature. The Hebrew not only recognized that He created the world but that His creative activity was continuous. God was directly behind every event in nature and there was no place in Hebrew minds for a series of secondary causes.[1] Since God was actively concerned with all His creation, it was natural for the Hebrews to recognize Him as the Supreme Sustainer of health.

In general, the Old Testament taught that good health resulted from holy living and was a divine gift of God. Healing of disease was likewise God's gift and was based on forgiveness, intercession, and sometimes sacrifice. The seeking of health from Yahweh was considered the definite duty of an individual.[2]

The point of greatest significance in the Hebrew concept of healing lies in the overall view of God's place in the healing process.

Let us look at selected passages which give us insight and information in these matters.

And it came to pass after these things, that one told Joseph, behond, thy father is sick: and he took with him his two sons, Manasseh and Ephraim. And one told Jacob, and said, behold, they son Joseph cometh unto thee: and Israel strengthened himself, and sat upon the bed (Gen. 48:1-2, KJV.)

This is the story of Joseph being summoned to go to the room of his sick father, Jacob. Jacob had been in Egypt for some seventeen years at the time of this report and he was 147 years old.

Joseph had ascended to the position of prime minister in Egypt with all the clout and wealth which that position offered.

Joseph was informed that his father was sick. Joseph took with him his two sons, Manasseh and Ephraim, as he went to visit his father and their grandfather.

Keep in mind what we said at the beginning of this chapter, that to be sick is to be weak, feeble, to be in bondage by some infirmity. Also recall that to visit is to give caring oversight once you have inspected or visited with the sick person.

When Jacob was told that his son Joseph was coming to see him, the Scripture states in verse two that Israel (Jacob) strengthened himself and sat upon the bed.

There are several insights I want to share with you to help us understand what it means to feed the sick.

First, to feed the sick sheep we must have information. Joseph was an administrative executive. He had power, influence, and wealth. He had people directly under him that were responsible to him to carry out the affairs of the nation, but Joseph did not have omnipresent ability. He had to be told that his father was sick.

In many church communities there are persons who are sick but no one knows about them. No one reports it to the pastor, deacons, minister of visitation, or whoever is responsible for making the visit.

To care properly for the sick sheep we must have information. Who they are and where they are is essential.

Second, Joseph made the visit. He came to caringly oversee the condition of his aging father.

Knowing of a person's sickness and knowing where the person is located is not sufficient in itself. We must move upon the information that we have.

Also notice Joseph's immediate reaction upon hearing of his father's sickness. Joseph no doubt had every reason to delay because there were other pressing matters. But he did not. He went to visit his father.

Third, look at the impact the anticipation of the visit had on Jacob. Joseph had not yet arrived, but in the hopeful anticipation that his son was coming helped in the healing process to strengthen Jacob. The text states that he sat upon the bed, which gives us the idea that he had been lying down. Hope helps in the healing process.

How well does the church today minister to feed the sick sheep who have fallen?

According to this Joseph-Jacob encounter there must be information and investigation which will lead to edification.

How many Jacobs would sit upon their beds and be strengthened if only they knew that Joseph was on his way?

And said, if thou wilt diligently hearken to the voice of the Lord thy God, and wilt do that which is right in his sight, and wilt give ear to his commandments, and keep all his statutes, I will put none of these diseases upon thee, which I have brought upon the Egyptians: for I am the Lord that healeth thee (Ex. 15:26, KJV).

The text is the word of the Lord given to the people of Israel as they came to the place called Marah. When they got to this place on their wilderness journey toward the Promised Land, the waters were bitter. The Lord showed Moses a tree which, when he threw it into the waters, made them become sweet.

It was at Marah that the Lord made a statute and an ordinance with the people and there proved them.

We have here at Marah a pre-Sinai enactment of the convenant and law that God would give concerning His people.

The Lord at this point took the initiative and entered these directives to His people.

Here are the main points of the proposal.

First, the people must diligently be attentive to the voice of the Lord their God.

Second, they must do that which is right in His sight.

Third, they must turn their ears to obey His commandments.

Fourth, they must keep all His statues.

If all these conditions were met, then the people would be beneficiaries of the promise. The Lord would put none of the diseases upon the people that He put upon the Egyptians. The reason is given in that the Lord is the One, the only One I might add, who heals them.

This passage is important in that it helps us understand the Hebraic mind set which understood all things as directly happening because of the Lord. There were no secondary causes. The Lord wounded or afflicted, and the Lord restored or healed.

To feed the sick who are among us, we need to understand that sickness—the wounded, the hurt, the bleeding, the mentally confused—has all come about because some statute or ordinance has been either broken or not fulfilled. I am not implying necessarily that people are sick because they have done something themselves that has made them sick. This is true in some cases but not true as a general rule. Why some people get sick and others do not cannot be easily explained from the human perspective.

What I do mean to say is that God has structured and ordered His world in such a way that there is a design and pattern that if followed will produce healthy individuals. When God created creation, He called on creation to create after its own kind. The creation that God had created was, by God's own analysis, good— very good. God did not program creation to produce unhealthy or sick persons. That it does occur is true but it was not in God's original design.

Going back to the text, the Israelites were told to understand that the diseases among them would come because of their disobedience in following and obeying God's statues and ordinances. Their healing would come because the Lord would do it.

People are sick today because somewhere, somehow, the plan and purpose that God has designed has malfunctioned. Why? Ultimately only God knows. What we do know is that for the sick person to recover, God has to do the healing. A bandage may not stop a cut from bleeding but the Balm in Gilead can.

And it came to pass after this, that Absalom the son of

David had a fair sister, whose name was Tamar; and
Amnon the son of David loved her. And Amnon was so
vexed, that he fell sick for his sister Tamar; for she was
a virgin; and Amnon thought it hard for him to do
anything to her ............................ (2 Sam. 13:1-2, KVJ).

## Sick for What Reason?

You must read through verse 14 to get the whole
story. David's son Absalom had a pretty sister whose
name as Tamar. David had another son named Amnon
who sexually desired Tamar. The Scripture states that
he desired her so much until he fell sick for her. There
is such a thing as love sickness and sickness unto evil,
for here we have a classic example.

Amnon was sick, but why? He was sick because he
desired above all else to fulfill his sexual desires for his
half sister.

If you read verse 6 of the aforementioned text, you
will discover that Amnon had made himself sick. This
was all a part of his scheme to seduce Tamar. He gave
the king instructions to have Tamar bring him a "cov-
ered" dish for the "sick"—all part of his devious plan.

Even when Tamar came with the requested "medicine" Amnon still refused to take it until he had the
scene just as he wanted it. Amnon did not want Tamar
to just bring the food and leave it, he wanted to eat it
out of her hand. Look at verse ten. It was at this point,
once Amnon had Tamar in his private bedroom, that he
forced himself upon her, raping her.

Amnon represents a lot of "sick people." They are
sick because of some evil desire or devilish intent. They
have made themselves sick because it is to their advantage to be sick. They are sick because of some sexual or
incestuous perversion.

Also notice to what extent these people will go to get

their way. Amnon had the nerve to instruct David, the
King of Israel. He also told the king what he needed to
get "well." Amnon was his own diagnostician and phar-
macist. He even knew what "doctor" could make him
well. In this case the doctor's name was Tamar.

As we go to feed the sick we must be aware of the
Amnons in this world—people who have made themselves sick. It is a fact that somewhere between forty
and fifty percent of the people who are classified as sick,
even to the extent of needing or requesting hospitalization, are not actually sick but have psychosomatic disorders. They believe they are sick, they want to be sick,
it is to their advantage to be sick.

Our Lord has told us to be as wise as serpents and as
harmless as doves. We must be aware when we encounter people who can tell us specifically what they need
in order to get well.

There are far too many Amnons on church sick lists
who wait to be waited on by some missionary circles or
who want the pastor's attention or time. This writer has
visited both the Brother Amnons and the Sister Amnons in this world. Beware!

> In those days was Hezekiah sick unto death. And the
> prophet Isaiah the son of Amoz came to him, and said
> unto him, Thus saith the Lord, Set thine house in order;
> for thou shalt die, and not live . . . (2 Kings 20:1-7, KJV).

Hezekiah, the King of Judah was sick. He was so sick
it was unto death. We would say he was on his deathbed
going down quickly. Death was not to be a surprise
invader to Hezekiah, so the Lord sent His mouthpiece
Isaiah down to the palace to tell King Hezekiah that he
was not going to recover, he was going to die.

Upon receiving the word, Hezekiah believed Isaiah

and turned his face toward the wall and prayed that it would not be as Isaiah had said.

From this Isaiah-Hezekiah encounter we get several biblical principles in how to minister to the sick, especially those whose illness is terminal.

First we have the report in verse 1 of chapter 20 that in those days Hezekiah was sick unto death. Here is the first principle. As we go to minister unto a sick person, we need to know for certain that the person is sick. Since we are creatures of time and are limited by what we can and cannot do, we need to prioritize our visitation schedule. This does not mean that all people are not important and that all sickness should not be ministered unto as best we can.

If a person is terminally ill and is at the point of death, we should certainly make this a high priority on our visitation schedule. With this type of person you may not have tomorrow. A person with a common cold would certainly not receive the same priority as a person with an incurable cancer.

The second principle we see from the text is that Isaiah went and visited King Hezekiah. The text states that Isaiah came to Hezekiah. This may sound and seem simple but it is not. Many people make mental and spirit visits. The mental visitors are those who imagine or see the person who is sick in their minds. They imagine or see themselves visiting with the sick person. Also the mental visitors are those who say to themselves, "I am going to visit so and so." The problem with the mental visitor is that the visit stays in the mind and never moves toward the presence of the sick person.

The spirit visitor is the person who identifies with the sick person, feels for her, wishes he could express to the sick just how he feels, wants her to know that he is thinking about her, hopes everything turns out okay.

The problem with this should be obvious. The sick person has not been visited.

Isaiah knew that King Hezekiah was sick unto death and he came unto him.

A third biblical principle we see from this passage is to bring a word from the Lord to the sick person. Sick room visitation is not the time nor place to bring the latest gossip. (I do not know of any time or place that is right for gossip). It is the time and place to bring the gospel. Our words may not be as forthright as Isaiah's were to Hezekiah, but we should share the Lord's word from the holy Scriptures with the sick.

The fourth principle is to accept the sickness for what it is and affirm the individual. Isaiah did not tell Hezekiah, "Do not worry about a thing. Just take it easy and in a few days you will be back on your feet as good as new." No! Isaiah told Hezekiah to set his house in order because he was not going to live—he was going to die. As we go as pastor or as caregivers, we should accept the sickness as it is and not pretend that it is not real. Most of the terminally ill persons I have visited and ministered unto wanted to know the truth about their situation. After the initial stages of why-me-it-is-not-so anger and rejection, they have wanted to talk openly and honestly about their condition. These times have been times of confession and recommitment to the Lord.

Fifth, we see that Isaiah, even though he told Hezekiah he would die and not live, did not say more than he was told to say. Isaiah did not tell Hezekiah that his situation was hopeless. Hezekiah was the one who turned toward the wall and prayed. In the middle of the court as Isaiah was leaving, the Lord sent him back in to Hezekiah, this time with the word that the Lord was going to extend his life fifteen years. The Lord was going to heal Hezekiah and on the third day Hezekiah was to go up unto the house of the Lord.

This is the sixth principle we get from this passage on how to feed the sick. Once the Lord has heard our prayers, answered them, given us healing and restoration, we should go up to the house of the Lord and be a living epistle to be read by the whole world that our God is able to deliver, to heal, to save, to make whole.

> And it came to pass in the month Nisan, in the twentieth year of Artaxerxes the king, that wine was before him: and I took up the wine, and gave it unto the king. Now I had not been beforetime sad in his presence. Wherefore the king said unto me, why is thy countenance sad, seeing thou art not sick? This is nothing else but sorrow of heart. (Neh. 2:1-2, KJV).

### Sickness from Broken Dreams

As Langston Hughes has asked, "What becomes of a dream deferred?" I want to add the second question, "What happens to the dreamer."

When we read the second chapter of Nehemiah we learn what happens to a dreamer whose dreams have been deferred, whose hopes reach no higher than the secret walls of his imagination.

Nehemiah was the cupbearer for King Artaxerxes. One day as he was serving the king, Nehemiah could not help but outwardly express the anguish of his soul on the canvas of his face.

"Why are you looking so sad," Artaxerxes asked Nehemiah. "You do not have any physiological symptons for your sickness. It must come from a broken spirit, a hurt heart."

Artaxerxes was right. Nehemiah had a shadow of sorrow over him because his heart was back in Jerusalem where he knew the city of his fathers was in ruins.

Nehemiah wanted to go back to reclaim and reestablish his ancestral rootage.

Artaxerxes granted Nehemiah his request and permitted him to go back home. Artaxerxes gave Nehemiah letters to bear him over as he went through the vast empire. You can read the story further into its development as Nehemiah encountered opposition but how he had a singlemindness to stay on the wall to complete the task. He kept a trowel in one hand and a sword in the other to defend himself from enemies.

I wonder how many Nehemiahs we encounter each day—people who are working in one occupation but who are sick because their ambition and aspiration is to be in another.

How many Nehemiahs have the sorrow of a broken heart who need to get a second opportunity to go back and start over again?

Sickness from broken dreams can destroy a person if they do not rethink their options, realign their possibilities with the present realities.

We can minister to such sick sheep if we would do one or all of the things which King Artaxerxes did. First, he was sensitive enough to recognize that there was something wrong with Nehemiah. Nehemiah was not a bad cupbearer—in fact, I am sure he was tops. That's no doubt one of the reasons he held the position. In Nehemiah's daily routine Artaxerxes was sensitive enough to recognize a problem. What care we would provide to people if we just realize they have a problem.

Second, Artaxerxes asked Nehemiah what was his problem. This is caring enough to get involved. Many people can recognize that something is bothering a person, but how many will actually move toward alleviating the problem?

Third, the king counseled Nehemiah on the specifics.

What are your requests? What do you see as a possible
solution to your problem? Most people have the answers to their own problems if they are asked the right
question. When Nehemiah responded to Artaxerxes,
his countenance lighted up, his courage rose, and his
confidence was regained.

Who are the Nehemiahs around you who are sick of
a broken heart because they are in one place desiring
to be in another? Who are at one station, career, or job
and really want to be in another? The next time you run
across one just remember what King Artaxerxes did in
Nehemiah's situation.

What becomes of a dream deferred? It will defer the
dreamer if it is not dealt with sufficiently.

> So went Satan forth from the presence of the Lord, and
> smote Job with sore boils from the sole of his foot unto
> his crown. And he took him a potsherd to scrape himself
> withal, and he sat down among the ashes. Then said his
> wife unto him, dost thou still retain thine integrity?
> Curse God, and die. But he said unto her, thou speaketh
> as one of the foolish women speaketh. What? Shall we
> receive good at the hand of God, and shall we not re-
> ceive evil? (Job 2:7-10, KJV).

### Sickness with Integrity

Perhaps you have heard the terms *death with dignity, euthanasia*—"mercy killing," *release therapy*. How
do you minister to a sick sheep (person) who has no
understanding of how or why their sickness has come
upon them? What do you say to a God-fearing, Christ-
loving, Holy Spirit-led man or woman who experiences
the misery of malady and the suffering and sorrow of
sickness? Job is a classic example. Is it better to die than
to endure the sickness? Look at Job. He can give you
answers.

Job was smote by Satan, but Job did not know this. He believed as all believers of his time—God was the primary cause, the only cause for what happened in a believer's life. If Job was well it was because the Lord had made him well. If Job was sick it was because the Lord had made him sick—no secondary or circumstantial causes.

How do you minister to a person that believes that his or her sickness is some kind of punishment? How do you feed someone with the word of the Lord when they believe their sickness has come as a result of not doing what the Lord commanded of them?

Job tells us a couple of things both to do and not do to keep our integrity in our sickness.

Job, after he was smitten by Satan with boils from the sole of his feet to the crown or top of his head, did not question God and did not accuse God. He did not even ask, "Why me, Lord?"

Job did none of these things. You know what Job did? He took a potsherd, a piece of broken pottery, and started to scratch himself and then he sat down among the ashes, a sign of sorrow and repentance.

Job's wife asked the penetrating, probing, pointed, personal question that sooner or later will come to all believers at some junction in their lives. Do you still maintain your integrity in God? Here is an exit, an alternate that will end it all. Curse God, go ahead and die. If you will permit me to contemporize this, Job's wife represents the school of thought which says, "What is the use? Stop taking the medicine; pull the plug and end it all. Life has no meaning or purpose. It's better to die with some sense of control and 'dignity' than to live with the uncertainties."

Job gives us good counseling medicine in how to help a sick person maintain personal integrity in the face of sickness. "Do what?" he said. "Shall we receive good at the hand of God, and shall we not receive evil?" Job was saying, "The Lord is in control of my health and my hurts. His hand regulates my thermostat and thusly He sets my temperature—not me, Thee."

In all of this Job did not sin with his lips. How many times have we heard the sick person sin with their lips—Why me? How come? What am I going to do? How will the bills get paid? What will my family and friends think of me? Will I be left alone?

How many times have we sinned with our lips in attempting to minister to a sick person? I know why you are in this condition. Your symptons are the same as my mother, father, sister, or brother. Just confess your sins and you will be okay. You need faith and this sickness will go away. It is not God's will for you to be sick, so you are not sick, you just think you are—and on and on and on it goes: sinning with our lips.

Job challenges all of us to have sickness with integrity and to minister to those who are sick with integrity.

> False witnesses did rise up; they laid to my charge things that I knew not. They rewarded me evil for good to the spoiling of my soul. But as for me, when they were sick, my clothing was sackcloth: I humbled my soul with fasting; and my prayer returned into mine own bosom (Ps. 35:11-13, KJV).

### Sick and Tired of the Sick

I just briefly wanted to mention this section from the Psalms because many times we will be called upon to minister to people who are sick, and who have caused us sickness or at least some discomfort or displeasure.

The psalmist so identified with those who had caused him grief until he put on the clothing of sackcloth.

He then told just what the people had done to him.
They had done false witness. They laid charges against
him that he knew nothing about. When he did good
they showed their appreciation by rewarding him with
evil. Yet when they became sick, he did not show them
contempt or refuse to minister unto them.

The psalmist stated in verse 14 that he behaved toward them as though they were his mother, brother, or
friend.

Perhaps there is a sick person whom you know has
mistreated you in the past, caused you real pain, hurt
and embarrassment. What will be your reaction to such
a sick sheep? I hope you will emulate the actions of the
psalmist. He saw their sickness as his own.

"Why should ye be stricken any more? Ye will revolt
more and more: the whole head is sick, and the whole
heart faint" (Isa. 1:5, KJV).

## Head Sickness

The word of the Lord was given to Isaiah to give to
the inhabitants of Judah and Jerusalem. The reason the
people walked in the wrong direction, spoke the wrong
words, behaved in an ungodly manner, saw with
blurred vision, and heard the lie rather than the truth
was because they had head sickness.

When you encounter a sheep with head sickness you
have a real situation on your hands.

I am not a psychiatrist nor a psychologist and I am not
about to attempt to go into all the mental disorders that
a person may have.

What I want to say to you who are attempting to feed
the sick sheep is to be on the alert. Cautiously be aware
that people with head sickness have a twisted theology,
a false perception of reality, a complex which believes
that the world is against them and they go from one

thing to another with no certainties in their lives. You
need to be on the alert for such because usually these
people need the joint care of a pastoral counselor and
a psychiatrist or other trained professionals in the mental health field.

> Is there no balm in Gilead; is there no physician there?
> Why then is not the health of the daughter of my people
> recovered (Jer. 8:22, KJV)?

Jeremiah, the prophet of the Lord, cried out in
lamentation when he realized that the harvesttime had
passed, the time of gathering the grain, and the sum-
mertime had passed, the time for gathering the fruit,
and yet his people were not saved. This speaks of the
tragedy of lost opportunities.

Jeremiah cried out in sorrow and with questions—Is
there no balm in Gilead? Is there no physician there?

The answer was certainly yes. Gilead was noted for
its medicinal herbs, the resin of the storax tree, and for
its physicians. The problem was not the availability of
a healing solution or practitioners to administer it. The
problem was one of application. The medicine and the
miserable ones were not meeting. The physician and
the pain kept eluding each other. The hospital and the
hurt never got together.

This is the tragedy of our times. God has sent His Son
into the world to save the world, to deliver the world,
to heal the world, to reconcile the world back unto
Himself, yet there still remains a great gap, a gulf if you
please, which keeps the Physician from ministering to
those who are perishing.

We need more compassionate prophets, preachers,
pastors like Jeremiah who will cry out and then move
to be an ambassador of healing reconciliation so the sick
sheep can be fed.

And the word of the Lord came unto me, saying, son of man, prophesy against the shepherds of Israel, prophesy and say unto them, thus saith the Lord God unto the shepherds; woe be to the shepherds of Israel that do feed themselves! Should not the shepherds feed the flocks? Ye eat the fat, and ye clothe you with the wool, ye kill them that are fed: but ye feed not the flock. The diseased have ye not strengthened, neither have ye healed that which was sick, neither have ye bound up that which was broken, neither have ye brought again that which was driven away, neither have ye sought that which was lost; but with force and with cruelty have ye ruled them. And they were scattered, because there is no shepherd: and they became meat to all the beasts of the field, when they were scattered. My sheep wandered through all the mountains, and upon every high hill: yea, my flock was scattered upon all the face of the earth, and none did search or seek after them (Ezek. 34:1-6, KJV).

### A Shepherd's Service to the Sick

In this final passage of our Old Testament Scriptures, look at how to feed the sick sheep. We have the words of the Lord given through His mouthpiece Ezekiel.

It is a word of condemnation upon the shepherds of Israel. What is the basis of the Lord's complaint against them? It is a sevenfold complaint.

1. The shepherds fed themselves instead of feeding the flock.
2. The shepherds took the wool from the sheep, clothing themselves but not the sheep.
3. The sheep are killed regularly but they are not fed regularly.
4. The diseased ones have not been cared for.
5. The sick have not been healed.

6. The straying sheep have not been sought and brought back to the flock.

7. The shepherds have driven the sheep instead of leading them.

The shepherds asked the Lord through Ezekial, When did we do all these things to You Lord? When You did not do unto the least of these? What will you answer when asked that question by the Good Shepherd?

### Biblical Perspectives: New Testament

In the days of His earthly ministry, Jesus' hands were even outstretched to heal.

Jesus came with an active compassion of intense spiritual energy and set about to give persons life in abundance. Healing power flowed out from Him like a stream of fresh water on the arid souls and tortured bodies of suffering humanity.[3] Matthew noted that in the very dawn of His ministry "Jesus went about all Galilee, teaching in their synagogues, and preaching the gospel of the kingdom, and healing all manner of sickness and all manner of disease among the people" (Matt. 4:23, KJV).

In no other realm in the ministry of the Master was His sovereignty as apparent as in His healing ministry. He was sovereign in the places He chose to visit and perform His power of healing. He asserted His sovereignty in regard to the people He chose to heal. He did not go everywhere and He did not heal everybody.[4]

Jesus healed for many and various reasons. The chief reason appears to be that Jesus wanted to reveal His divine person, power, and His ultimate purpose and mission. He had come to make the wounded whole, to liberate the oppressed, to set at liberty those in captivity.

Jesus also healed to validate His personal claims of His messiahship. Jesus said repeatedly, "If you do not believe Me because of words, then believe Me because of My works." His healing ministry was a validation that the kingdom of God had come and was breaking the old bondage of sin and shame.

And finally we see in the healing ministry of Jesus parabolic illustrations of His ultimate purpose of complete redemption of all who came to Him by faith. The healings of Jesus were never done as ends in themselves. They always pointed to a greater reality, a greater realism that the power, promises, and presence of God were upon the scene.

We will now look briefly at selected passages of the healing ministry of Jesus and from these passages discover—by the guidance of the Holy Spirit—means and methods of how to feed the sick.

We will then focus our attention upon selected passages from Acts, then the Epistles, and say a concluding word from Revelation.

> And Jesus went about all Galilee, teaching in their synagogues, and preaching the gospel of the kingdom, and healing all manner of sickness and all manner of disease among the people.
> And his fame went throughout all Syria: and they brought unto him all sick people that were taken with divers diseases and torments, and those which were possessed with devils, and those which were lunatick, and those that had the palsy: and he healed them (Matt. 4:23-24, KJV).

From this passage we see the magnitude of Jesus' healing ministry. Jesus was a healing specialist. He healed *all* kinds of diseases and sickness. No case was out of His realm of expertise. Jesus healed all chronic and serious diseases. He healed all occasional illnesses among the people. He healed those who were in a miserable condition physically, suffering with various kinds of chronic and serious ailments and acute pain. He healed those who were demonized, epileptic, and paralytic.

Jesus healed not as an addition or an attachment to His messianic ministry. The scripture states that as He was going about preaching the gospel of the Kingdom and teaching in their synagogues, he was healing all manner of sickness and disease among the people.

Let us list some of these biblical principles from which we can develop a model of feeding the sick among us.

In our ministry to the sick we should be preaching and teaching the gospel of the Kingdom. Healing for Jesus was never separated from preaching or teaching. He never healed the physically ill just to heal the physically ill. Jesus' healing always pointed to a deeper spiritual reality. His healing was a demonstration, a declaration, a demanding confrontation that the kingdom of God had come.

As we go to minister to the sick sheep we should always be preaching and teaching the gospel. If you separate the preaching and teaching ministries from the healing ministry one might be led to believe that we have been healed for ourselves. We are not healed for ourselves. We are healed for God's glory.

Second, we learn from this passage that we must not be selective or segregative in our ministry approach. Jesus dealt with the temporarily sick, the chronically sick, the physically handicapped, the mentally drained, the demon possessed, those who were tormented, and He healed all of them.

I grant you there are various approaches one should take in ministering to various persons with different

illnesses. The point here is that as disciples of Jesus
Christ we have a responsibility to minister to all of
them.

Allow me to give you some ministry methods in visiting and caring for various types of sick situations.

## Methods for Visiting the Sick at Home

1. Inform the person that you are coming. You are
   going as a caregiver into the privacy of a person's
   home. You want to respect that home as such.
2. Be sensitive to the home situation. Do not go in and
   rearrange their furniture. You did not come to
   redecorate their house; you came to minister to
   them.
3. Keep the visit a visit. You have come to bring the
   glorious gospel, not the gory gossip.
4. Keep your personal health problems to yourself. If
   I am sick it does not make me feel better to know
   you are, too.
5. Visit in twos. This is especially wise when visiting
   members of the opposite sex who live alone and
   who are of various ages. You have to work at
   removing all appearances of evil. (see I Thess. 5:-
   22.)
6. Have a word of prayer and appropriate Scripture
   reading if permitted. I say "permitted" because
   some persons will interpret your prayer with them
   as your belief that they are dying and that you will
   not make it back before they are dead. You have to
   be sensitive. If you read Scripture, select an appropriate passage, Psalms 23, 27, 46, Matthew 5:9-13,
   Romans 8:31-39, just to name a few.
7. Future visits. Only announce your intentions of
   coming back if you really plan on coming back. Be
   cautious of giving a specific day or time unless you

honestly plan on keeping it. The sick person at home has nothing to do but wait on your return visit.

## Methods of Visiting the Shut-in

In this visitation situation you are going in an attempt to minister to the person who is confined, hoping to prevent the individual from becoming a "shut-out."

1. Establish a pattern of visitation. You may decide on a certain day of the week to visit only shut-in persons.
2. Build a relationship. Inform them of events that are of interest to them.
3. Refer them to outside avenues of ministry interest —quality television programs, religious radio broadcasts, cassette tapes, magazines, church bulletins and newsletters. You may want to look into the purchase or rental of videocassette equipment to show these programs on their home television set.
4. Do not appear to be in a hurry. Make a visit when you really have time to visit. The shut-in person has nowhere to go and so you have to be sensitive to their world.
5. Remember them at special times—birthdays, anniversaries, church events, socials, holidays. Put their names on special programs or bulletins and send them to them. This way they are included in outside activities.

## Methods for Visiting the Hospitalized

Your objective is to go to offer loving care to the hospitalized person. You should be aware of all the many reasons people are hospitalized. All are not there because they are seriously ill. Some are there for major surgery and some are there for minor tests.

1. Check with the nurse or knock lightly before entering the hospital room.
2. Go as a caregiver, not as a person investigating the reason for the person's hospitalization.
3. Do not ask, "What is the problem?" or "What is the matter?" It is none of your business. And even if you knew, what can you medically do about it?
4. Keep the visit a visit. Do not go as a reporter, especially of all that is bad or wrong in the world. Most definitely do not tell a hospitalized person how sick someone else is or who just died.
5. Have a word of prayer or read a passage of Scripture. Keep in mind that Jesus was preaching and teaching while he was healing.

**Some Don'ts in Hospital Visitation**

Don't:
1. Stay too long. You are a visitor, not a resident of the hospital. You are there to visit, not to entertain or occupy the room.
2. Talk of sickness as God's punishment. You do not know why the person is sick.
3. Sit on the side of the bed. This could be painful and is quite unsanitary.
4. Smoke in the room. This could be unwise, especially if oxygen is in use or is an offense to the other patient.
5. Tell the person how you have been trying to get to the hospital but just now were able to do it. Don't tell the person you were in the neighborhood or out this way and thought while you had some free time you would stop in.

6. Tell them not to worry about a thing. You do not know all of the "things" they have to deal with.
7. Tell them when you are coming back unless you really plan on keeping that appointment.

### Methods for Visiting in a Mental Institution

"He asked him, 'What is thy name?' and he answered, saying, 'my name is legion; for we are many' " (Mark 5:9).

1. Go as one seeking to feed the mentally sick. You are not a psychiatrist, psychologist, or psychoanalyst.
2. Be at your best mental health before you go to visit. Do not be anxious or anxiety ridden. Slow down by praying, thinking on a verse of Scripture. Anticipate what to expect and how to react.
3. Affirm the person but do not become argumentative. Depending on the state of the mental illness, this person may say anything or do anything. Usually they will not harm you. If this is a possibility you probably will not be allowed to see the person.
4. Silence is good therapy. You have to move away from the idea that you have to *say* something to *do* something.
5. Be prepared for confessions and prayer requests. Be sensitive in your listening and if you should pray, be specific and brief, using the Scriptures as your words.
6. Do not try to identify with the person by telling them you have thought the same thoughts or have done the same things.

These methods are but a few of the many ways that you can develop into being a caregiver for people who are sick whether at home, hospital, shut-in, or institutionalized for whatever reason.

Jesus, our Lord, went to all types of people and He ministered unto them. We cannot afford to do anything less if we truly love Him.

"But when Jesus heard that, he said unto them, They that be whole need not a physician, but they that are sick" (Matt. 9:12, KJV).

Jesus was in Matthew Levi's house, the tax collector. The Pharisees questioned Jesus' disciples concerning the company Jesus was keeping. Jesus' reply to their question was, they are sick and I am a physician. A physician should be where there is sickness.

The point for our emphasis from this passage is that Jesus took the initiative in coming to Matthew Levi's house.

If we are to minister to feed the sick then we must take the initiative. We must also be aware of and prepared for the criticism and even opposition we may encounter.

"And Jesus went forth, and saw a great multitude, and was moved with compassion toward them, and he healed their sick" (Matt. 14:14, KJV).

### Crowds and Compassion

How do you view the crowds? Do you look upon the crowd with contempt, disgust, or indifference? When Jesus saw the crowd, He was moved with compassion. His inner being, his inner bowels if you please—for that is what the word *compassion* means in the Greek—was moved to the point of doing something about it.

Our problem is not that we do not have the means or medicine to heal or help the sick, nor is the problem a lack of the crowd who needs us. Our problem is that, too often, we do not have compassion.

This was the problem Jesus said would lead to our condemning judgment. "When saw we sick Lord?" Jesus replies "Everytime you saw the crowd, the sick, the lame, the mentally confused—you saw Me."

Do you see the multitude? They need the medicine of the gospel. Jesus said to feed them. "Heal the sick, cleanse the lepers, raise the dead, cast out the devils; freely ye have received, freely give" (Matt. 10:8, KJV).

### Commissioned to Care

Jesus sent His twelve disciples out with authority and assurance. Jesus commissioned them to care for the sick. They were to cleanse the lepers, raise the dead, cast out devils. Freely they had received, freely they were to give.

As disciples of Jesus Christ, we have been given that same commission.

The next time you see a sick person, go to minister to them. If you are asked what you are doing and why you are doing it, tell them you are under orders to do what you are doing to the least of them.

"Now a certain man was sick, named Lazarus, of Bethany, the town of Mary and her sister Martha" (John 11:1-7, KJV).

### Responding to a Sick Request

Jesus had been informed about Lazarus' sickness, but He did not move immediately. He waited two more days and then went to Bethany. By this time Lazarus had died. Why did Jesus wait? What caused Him to delay? Jesus said that the reason He waited was so that the Son of God would be glorified.

You will often be called upon to respond to a sick situation. Sometimes you will be able to move swiftly, sometimes you will not. Make sure that as you move, you move so the Son of God can be glorified. All sickness is not unto death. Some is and some is not. You can neither prevent the sickness or the death. Your task will be to minister, no matter what the outcome.

> Insomuch that they brought forth the sick into the streets, and laid them on beds and couches, that at least the shadow of Peter passing by might overshadow some of them (Acts 5:15, KJV).

Miracles and wonders were being performed in Jerusalem. The people were aware of God's presence among His people. The people went and got those who were sick, the shut-ins, the chronically ill and brought them out into the street so that at least the shadow of Peter might fall on them, because they needed deliverance the most.

There are many sick people today who need someone to just go and get them and bring them to the "Peters." Many shut-ins could come to worship services at church if someone would go and get them, if proper provisions would be made for them. There are many sick people who have surrendered to their sickness instead of fighting for health. There are those on beds and couches who need to be told to get up, that their situations are not helpless.

"Erastus abode at Corinth: but Trophimus have I left at Miletum sick" (2 Tim. 4:20, KJV).

Paul, in his closing farewell to Timothy gave him a personal report on some of the companions who were with him. Trophimus was left at Miletum sick.

This is a word which needs to be sounded to people who want us to believe that it is ungodly or outside of God's will to be sick.

Since Paul was the Lord's apostle, why did he not cure Trophimus of his sickness? Why did Paul have the thorn in his flesh remain with him if all he had to do was believe and it would go away?

This is a word from the Word that some will be sick and some will remain sick. Even though they are in the Lord's service, in God's will, have received God's blessing, some will remain at Miletum sick.

> Is any sick among you? let him call for the elders of the church; and let them pray over him, anointing him with oil in the name of the Lord: and the prayer of faith shall save the sick, and the Lord shall raise him up; and if he have committed sins, they shall be forgiven him (Jas. 5:14-15, KJV).

The text refers to the sickness that comes as to a sinning brother who is being disciplined by the Lord. If a person is sick, he is to call for the elders of the church. They are to anoint with oil. This is a reference to the use of medicinal intervention along with the prayer of faith. The prayer of faith is to pray in accordance with God's will. When and if healing happens, it will happen because God has healed the person.

This passage helps us understand several factors about the ministry to feed the sick.

First, there should be the confession of sin to keep open the channel of God's blessings. Some of our sickness has come as a direct result of sins we have committed.

Second, those in the body of Christ should be ministered unto by those in the fellowship. The elders, pastors, and deacons are to be called as instruments in God's healing process.

Third, anointing with oil or the use of medicinal procedures. It is not a matter of either/or but both/and —God and medicine. Both faith and prescriptions are to be used. All healing ultimately comes from the Lord.

Fourth, healing of the physically sick is never done just for the healing of the physically sick. God has His purpose in our healing as a witness for His glory. The church is edified and God is glorified when a sick person is restored to health.

> And God shall wipe away all tears from their eyes; and there shall be no more death, neither sorrow, nor crying, neither shall there be any more pain: for the former things are passed away.
>
> In the midst of the street of it, and on either side of the river, was there the tree of life, which bare twelve manner of fruits, and yielded her fruit every month: and the leaves of the tree were for the healing of the nations (Rev. 21:4; 22:2, KJV).

The hope for the believer is that there is coming a day when the pain, sickness, and sorrow of this world will pass away.

In the first text from Revelation, we have the assurance that God Himself shall wipe away the tears. He shall remove the presence of pain.

In the second text there is the word of assurance that in the New Jerusalem there will be a tree where leaves are for the healing of the nations.

Sickness and sorrow may endure for the night, but joy does come in the morning (see Ps. 30:5).

Jesus said, "If you love Me, feed My sheep."

Feed My sick sheep.

# 6
# Feeding the Prisoner

*I was in prison and you came to visit me (Matt. 25:36, NIV).*

In this final chapter, we will consider the words of our Lord and Savior when He said, "I was in prison and you came to visit Me."

A brief survey of the biblical record reveals that prisons were varied and diverse. They could be anything from chains, a pit, dungeon, stocks, guardhouse, any kind of restraint, bonds, cells, jail, house arrest, court of the guard, and just plain prisons.

The American Correctional Association estimates that there are over six thousand correctional and detention centers in this country. There are over five hundred thousand people incarcerated at any given time, with as many as three million men, women, and children passing through the correctional facilities at any given time. In conjunction with the federal, state, and local prisons and jails, there are halfway houses, work-release centers, juvenile-detention centers, reformatories, prison hospitals, and other types of confinement facilities.

It is almost too obvious, but allow me to say it. The church must have a viable ministry that grows in proportion to the needs of those who are prison-bound.

What we want to do in this chapter is to get biblical perspectives from the Old and New Testaments and,

from these biblical passages, get biblical principles that
will help us develop ministry strategies to go to those
who are in prison.

### Biblical Perspectives—Old Testament

> So when Joseph came to his brothers, they stripped him
> of his robe—the richly ornamented robe he was wear-
> ing—and they took him and threw him into the cistern.
> Now the cistern was empty; there was no water in it.
> (Gen. 37:23-24, NIV).

This first biblical reference of "prison," in this case a
cistern where Joseph was placed, gives us insight and
information about the place of incarceration.

Joseph was placed there because of the jealousy of his
brothers. He had not wronged them or done anything
offensive to anybody. Can you just imagine travelers
passing by that way, seeing Joseph in that cistern-pris-
on, and concluding he was there because he deserved
to be. That would have been tragic and, yet, we do the
same thing when we see someone under arrest, in jail,
or in prison. We almost automatically conclude they
deserve to be there. Well, Joseph did not, and certainly
there are hundreds if not thousands of others like him.

The cistern normally held rainwater, but the one
Joseph was placed in was empty. There was no water
in it. To be incarcerated is to be empty, to be where
there is an absence, no water, inadequate provisions.

If we seriously seek ways to minister to those who are
in prison, there are some biblical principles for giving
us strategies to minister.

First, do not conclude that all incarcerated persons
are guilty of some crime. This is not true.

Second, those who are incarcerated are empty. This
emptiness can be the result of injustice, mistreatment,

not valuing human life, not respecting the property of
others, wrong self-image, distorted view of reality; the
list could go on endlessly, but the basic point is there is
an emptiness.

Third, there is no water. There are needs that can be
met. This "water" can manifest itself in legal aid and
counseling, financial assistance, spiritual counseling
and direction, confessional and admittance of guilt and
sin, reality therapy, person-to-person relationships, or
just knowing that someone cares.

> Joseph's master took him and put him in prison, the
> place where the king's prisoners were confined. But
> while Joseph was there in the prison, the Lord was with
> him; he showed him kindness and granted him favor in
> the eyes of the prison warden. So the warden put Joseph
> in charge of all those held in the prison, and he was
> made responsible for all that was done there. The ward-
> en paid no attention to anything under Joseph's care
> because the Lord was with Joseph and gave him success
> in whatever he did (Gen. 39:20-23, NIV).

If you read the entire thirty-ninth chapter of Genesis,
you will have the whole story as to why Joseph was
placed in prison. This time it was because of Potiphar's
wife who was pursuing him to have sexual relations. He
fled from her presence but she grabbed hold of his
outer garment and presented this as evidence to her
husband.

Once again, it had been a garment which had gotten
Joseph in trouble.

This time Joseph was placed not in solitary confinement but in the company of the king's prisoners. The
Lord was also with Joseph in this ordeal. The keeper of
the prison—or as we would refer to him, the warden—
favored Joseph and gave him the charge of overseeing

the other prisoners and, from the text, we can understand he had freedom in running the prison. The reason
is clearly given for this flexibility while in confinement:
the Lord was with him.

The biblical principle for our ministry strategy is
once again not to prejudge that all who are incarcerated are guilty. I do not want to leave you with the impression that there are not some, or should I say many,
persons incarcerated who are guilty and belong in prison. Joseph just did not belong there.

The Lord can use persons who are classified as prisoners or convicts to present His compassionate and life-
converting message of the gospel. Joseph was given
charge over the other prisoners. Think what influence
his godly character must have had over the other prisoners.

The Lord's work can be effectively carried on by
prisoners to proclaim the gospel and care for those who
are in like predicaments. As a pastor, minister, servant
in the Lord's business, we can equip those who are
incarcerated to minister to others. An insider can, in
many instances, be more effective than an outsider.

> Then the Philistines seized him, gouged out his eyes,
> and took him down to Gaza. Binding him with bronze
> shackles, they set him to grinding in the prison (Judg.
> 16:21, NIV).

This biblical passage refers to Samson after he had
divulged the secret of his strength to Delilah.

His imprisonment came as a result of the crime he
had committed by telling Delilah the secret of his
strength. The cruelty of his captors is seen in their
putting out his eyes. He was made to work with shack-
les of brass, blinded by their torture.

How many prisoners have been tortured? Police brutality, jailers' abuse, guards' unnecessary roughness—all can be documented. This is not to say that these persons are not guilty of the crime of which they have been convicted; it is to say they are still human beings who should be treated in a humane fashion.

How many incarcerated persons' eyes are out? They do not see themselves as made in God's image; they do not see other persons as creatures of infinite worth; they do not see that their actions will lead to their self-destruction. They do not see there is another way. How will they see unless someone speaks to their silence? How will they repent unless they are presented a sin-pardoning Savior? Until, and unless, this happens, they will continually grind in the prison house.

> In the thirty-seventh year of the exile of Jehoiachin, king of Judah, in the year Evil-Merodach became king of Babylon, he released Jehoiachin from prison on the twenty-seventh day of the twelfth month. He spoke kindly to him and gave him a seat of honor higher than those of the other kings who were with him in Babylon. So Jehoiachin put aside his prison clothes and for the rest of his life ate regularly at the king's table. Day by day, the king gave Jehoiachin a regular allowance as long as he lived (2 Kings 25:27-30, NIV).

This segment of Scripture could be labeled, "How to Minister to Former Prisoners Once They Are Paroled or Released."

The historical context briefly stated is often the first seige of Jerusalem in 612 BC by Nebuchadnezzer of Babylon and then the second seige in 587 BC. During this period of conquering and capturing, vassal kings were placed upon the throne in Judah. The men of valor and persons of prominence were carried away in the Babylonian Exile. When Evil-Merodach became king of Babylon, he released Jehoiachin, king of Judah, out of prison.

The salvation history of God's providence was probing and penetrating the plunder and perplexity that the people of God presently found themselves. In the midst of it all, God was still in control, working His pleasurable purposes.

For our purposes, let us look at the moves Evil-Merodach made in the rehabilitation of Jehoiachin, the king of Judah, who was a prisoner.

First, he spoke kindly to him. He related to him in a person of importance and worthy way. He did not demoralize or depersonalize Jehoiachin just because he was his prisoner. In the language of Martin Buber, he related to Jehoiachin as a person, not as an "it."

What a ministry strategy we need to learn in ministering to those who are incarcerated! They may or may not be guilty of the crime as convicted, this we may not know absolutely; but there is one thing we always know absolutely, and that is they are persons made in the image of God and thus are of infinite worth. How many fights and even wars could have been avoided? How many counseling sessions may never have been needed, if only someone had spoken kindly to the other? As we go to minister in our Lord's name, let us keep this biblical principle before us in relating and reaching the prisoners; speak kindly to them.

Second, Evil-Merodach gave Jehoichin a seat of honor higher than the other kings who were with him in Babylon. This seat business has to do with position, prominence, power, and restoration. He not only released Jehoiachin, he restored him.

The biblical principle for us is, after justification (acquittal), there must follow reconciliation (rehabilitation). To just tell a man or woman who has been in jail or prison that they are free to go without directing them *where* to go and *how* to get there is often fruitless and futile.

Third, Jehoichin put aside his prison garments. To change one's garments in this sense is to change one's robe, one's relationship, one's responsibility. As long as Jehoiachin had on prison clothes, he was seen as a prisoner, treated as a prisoner, and no doubt thought of himself as a prisoner. Keep in mind that he was king of Judah, but he had on prison clothes. Persons who are paroled or released from jail or prison need to change their "clothes."

Fourth, the text states, "and for the rest of his life ate regularly at the king's table. Day by day, the king gave Jehoiachin a regular allowance as long as he lived."

Evil-Merodach provided Jehoiachin with perpetual care. He not only released him, redressed him, but he daily gave him provisions.

It is one thing to make a jail or prison visit, you know, the ten-to-twenty minute kind, it is something radically different to provide a ministry of extended care to those who are there, released, or to their families.

Evil-Merodach provided for Jehoiachin all the days of his life. We may not have the means to minister that extensively, but we certainly can refer both the former and present prisoners to the Good Shepherd who has promised that goodness and mercy will follow us all the days of our lives.

For the Lord heareth the poor, and despiseth not his prisoners (Ps. 69:33, KJV).

May the groans of the prisoners come before you;
by the strength of your arm,
preserve those condemned to die (Ps. 79:11, NIV).

The Lord looked down from his sanctuary on high,
from heaven he viewed the earth,
to hear the groans of the prisoners
and release those condemned to death (Ps. 102:19-20,
   NIV).

Set me free from my prison,
that I may praise your name.
Then the righteous will gather about me
because of your goodness to me (Ps. 142:7, NIV).

These four passages from the Psalter speak specifically concerning the confident pleading of the psalmist putting his trust in God's compassion concerning his condition and God's power to deliver.

The lament of sorrow and regret is expressed in all four passages. The prison is understood, whether literally or symbolically, as whatever has placed restraints, caused confinement, and restricted freedom and movement in the life of the individual. The basis of the petitions is God's gracious goodness and everlasting mercy.

The enemy may be the Babylonians who have conquered the city, or the burdens of daily problems that have served to crush the tranquillity of the person. The result is the same—prison.

The purpose of the petition is made clear in the last passage selected, Psalm 142:7; "Set me free from my prison that I may praise your name." I do not want release for release's sake, I want release so I can rejoice in the God of my salvation. I want to be released as a witness to God's goodness. I wonder how many persons are in jail or prison at this present moment who want to be released so they can praise the Lord?

Passages such as these can help us in our ministering to the prisoners by transforming what seemingly is a stumbling block into a stepping-stone by God's grace, getting the prisoners to understand that only the Lord can truly set them free and that their mission and message, once release has been granted, is to be a witness to God's goodness.

> I, the Lord, have called you in righteousness;
> I will take hold of your hand.
> I will keep you and will make you
> to be a covenant, for the people
> and a light for the Gentiles,
> to open eyes that are blind, to free captives from prison,
> and to release from the dungeon those who sit in darkness (Isa. 42:6-7, NIV).

This passage, taken from Deutero-Isaiah, reflects the mission, message, and ministry that God's people are to have as God's servant. The key thought is what the Lord was going to do with His people. Listen to it: "I, the Lord, have called you in righteousness; I will make you . . . a light." The point is I, the Lord, will do this. The Lord will use His people to accomplish His redemptive task.

That task is explicit. Open the eyes that are blind, free captives from prison, and release from the dungeon those who sit in darkness.

Since God's word did not change the ministry task for His people then, it is the ministry task for His people now. The Lord has called us to be "a chosen people; a royal priesthood, a holy nation, a people belonging to God, that [we] may declare the praises of him who called [us] out of darkness into his wonderful light (1 Pet. 2:9, NIV).

> He was taken from prison and from judgment: and who shall declare his generation? for he was cut off out of the land of the living: for the transgression of my people was he stricken (Isa. 53:8, KJV).

In keeping with the suffering motif elaborated upon in the previous verse, this reference is to the Suffering Servant. The promise of the Messiah for those in Isaiah's day was that He would come and deliver those in bondage, binding up their wounds, redeeming them. We who live on the resurrection side of this story know that the Messiah has come; Jesus the Christ. Surely He bore our grief and carried our sorrows. The Scripture says of him, "For he hath made him to be sin for us, who knew no sin; that we might be made the righteouness of God in him" (2 Cor. 5:21, KJV). He became what we are, that we might become what He is.

For us to minister efficiently and effectively, we will have to be suffering servants. We will have to identify with the pain and anguish, we will have to go where they are, and meet with them in the name of our Christ. Remote control will not suffice. Only an incarnational ministry of flesh and blood will do it.

> The Spirit of the Sovereign Lord is on me,
> because the Lord has anointed me
> to preach good news to the poor.
> He has sent me to bind up the brokenhearted,
> to proclaim freedom for the captives
> and release for the prisoners,
> to proclaim the year of the Lord's favor
> and the day of vengeance of our God,
> to comfort all who mourn (Isa 61:1-2, NIV).

This selection refers to Isaiah's ministry of deliverance. The Spirit of the Lord had anointed, so endowed, and filled Him, that he must go with the power and presence of the Spirit to bring good news to the despondent, whether they be the poor, the brokenhearted, the captives, or the prisoners.

Isaiah's task was to speak the word into their ears that

they might know that their God was able and will deliver. To see the people downtrodden and full of despair must be met with the uplifting word that their Lord reigns. The wounded must hear and come to know their God is a healer. The prisoner and captive must know their God is a liberator and reconciler.

From this selection, we get a biblical principle of ministry strategy—we have been anointed and sent by the Sovereign Lord. Our ministry will be evident in our message of deliverance. Within the wildernesses of brokenness, captivity, and prison situations must be a voice speaking hope and healing.

Our problem is not an optical one of not seeing, ours is a vocal one of not speaking. See, and then speak; speak, and then serve.

It is our Father's will that none should perish; whoever they are, wherever they may be.

So they took Jeremiah and put him into the cistern of Malkijah, the king's son, which was in the courtyard of the guard. They lowered Jeremiah by ropes into the cistern; it had no water in it, only mud; and Jeremiah sank down into the mud. But Ebed-Melech, a Cushite, an official in the royal palace, heard that they had put Jeremiah into the cistern. While the king was sitting in the Benjamin Gate, Ebed-Melech went out of the palace and said to him, "My Lord, the king, these men have acted wickedly in all they have done to Jeremiah, the prophet. They have thrown him into a cistern, where he will starve to death when there is no longer any bread in the city" (Jer. 38:6-9, NIV).

This is only one of many instances where Jeremiah was thrown in prison or confinement for preaching the truth. He constantly kept telling the king and the people that their capture was inevitable, and their best defense was surrender. This irritated the king and his

military advisers; and thus Jeremiah was placed in prison—in this specific case, a cistern.

Ebed-Melech, a eunuch in the king's court, heard of
the plot against Jeremiah and went to the king seeking
his release. Ebed-Melech made a humanitarian appeal
that Jeremiah would perish in the cistern because there
was no food there. Second, Ebed-Melech pursued the
king in this matter of Jeremiah's release in that the men
who had placed him there had acted wickedly, with
injustice. Third, it could be inferred that Jeremiah had
done nothing wrong. He had spoken the truth and thus
the truth was its own defense.

These appeals moved the king to grant Ebed-Melech
permission to secure Jeremiah's release.

We can get several strategies for prison ministry from
this Scripture segment.

First, all persons who are incarcerated are not guilty
of some wrong. Many are there because of the right
they have done. One does not always get justice in a
court of law. In fact, the law may be observed, but
justice may not be obeyed.

Jeremiah certainly had done no wrong. He spoke the
truth as the Lord gave it to him. He had not, however,
received the prophet-preacher award for the year.

Second, we who are seeking to minister to the prison-
bound should work to see that the prison environment
is as humane as it should be. A person guilty or innocent
is still a person of infinite worth. Just the public visiting
jails and prisons will help to some degree to make sure
the prison personnel are keeping the living conditions
up to some standard of decency.

Jeremiah was placed in a cistern and lowered into the
mud—no place for a prophet or a pauper.

Third, appeals can and should be made for prison
reform on at least two levels—the first at the

humanitarian level and second, at the justice level. If one person acts inhumanly, that does not justify another person to react inhumanly.

Ebed-Melech was moved to do something about Jeremiah's situation on the human front.

Justice is another motivator to get persons actively involved with those who are in prison. In far too many instances, justice has not been done because the person did not have enough money, proper legal counsel, or enough persons of reputation to witness in his/her defense.

In verse 11 of chapter 38, the Scripture tells us that Ebed-Melech went to secure some men and "some old rages and worn-out clothes" and used the garments to pad the ropes under Jeremiah's arms. The men were the source of strength to pull Jeremiah out of the cistern.

We will have to go and get what we can and use it to God's glory, pulling and tying, minding and fixing how we can see that humanity be served and justice be executed in Jesus' name.

In this brief Old Testament survey, we have looked at persons in prison, starting with Joseph down to Jeremiah. We have expounded upon selected biblical passages and from them, have developed ministry strategies to help us in prison ministry.

We now focus our attention upon the New Testament perspective to get a better understanding of what our Lord meant when He said, "I was in prison and you came to visit Me."

## New Testament Perspective

"When Jesus heard that John had been put in prison, he returned to Galilee." (Matt. 4:12, NIV). This is a significant starting point as we survey selected passages in the New Testament concerning prison ministry.

Matthew records that it was the decisive moment of John the Baptist's imprisonment that prompted Jesus to move out in His ministry. Knowing that John had received persecution; namely, imprisonment because he told Herod Antipas it was not lawful for him to have his brother's wife, Jesus began to move out preaching that the kingdom of heaven was at hand.

John the Baptist's imprisonment can be seen as a "motivator" to Jesus that it was now the time to begin his public ministry of announcing the inbreaking of the kingdom of heaven in human affairs.

As we minister to persons who are in prison, it can be the decisive motivator to inspire us to develop our skills for ministry. Many persons may have not entered the legal profession because of having to deal with legal jargon and court proceedings.

Intense Bible study has helped individuals who have had to develop special skills in Christian counseling, taking the techniques of psychology and social therapy, and bringing them in conjunction with biblical truth.

Social ministries have come about as persons sought to aid the families of incarcerated persons and, even in the process of placing paroled or released prisoners, Christian social approaches have been developed.

Prayer groups, mission-minded groups, and prison fellowships have all come about because someone who was incarcerated served as the motivator to move others into action.

> Settle matters quickly with your adversary who is taking you to court. Do it while you are still with him on the way, or he may hand you over to the judge, and the judge may hand you over to the officer, and you may be

thrown into prison. I tell you the truth, you will not get
out until you have paid the last penny (Matt. 5:25-26,
NIV).

This passage is the word of Jesus to His disciples concerning how they were to move swiftly to make reconciliation with someone to whom they owed a debt. The
possibility was that they might be placed in debtor's
prison. Once this happened, there was almost no opportunity of getting out until the final payment had been
made.

This biblical principle could serve as a ministry
strategy for us in preprison ministries. What ministry
do we offer persons who have been accused of some
crime? Do we take the constitutional approach, "innocent until proven guilty"? Or do we conclude that if
charged, they must be guilty?

Many persons in Christian communities who have to
encounter some type of police restraint, arrest, or have
to make a court appearance, are often looked upon
with a "do not touch" attitude. These persons need the
love, understanding, and support of the Christian community more than ever before.

What about the individuals in the larger community
who are charged with crimes who do not have the
means to secure the best legal counsel available? Many
times, court-appointed lawyers are aggravated because
they have the case, let alone trying to find a just solution. Could not the church provide legal counsel,
through pooling the resources together? What about
some of the lawyers who belong to many churches giving some time and advice as a part of their Christian
witness? Financially, in many cases, it is cheaper to
keep a person out of prison than it is to pay for their

daily upkeep. Why not work to see what kind of reconciliation can take place before the imprisonment?

"But he refused. Instead, he went off and had the
man thrown into prison until he could pay the debt"
(Matt. 18:30 NIV). This verse comes in a comparative
parable Jesus told concerning a king who had a servant
who owed him much. The king was merciful and extended the credit and gave the servant opportunity to
repay what he owed without suffering the inevitable
consequences. This forgiven servant had a fellow servant who owed him a small amount and yet he requested him to pay in full. He was so outraged that the
servant did not or could not pay him that he had him
thrown into prison until he could pay the debt.

The word for us in this parable is "forgiveness."
Christians are good at articulating the word *forgiveness,* but seemingly have an impossible penchant to
forgive. There is much talk of forgiveness, but often the
thought is on revenge.

As we move in prison ministries, we must learn and
execute the biblical principle of forgiveness. Regardless
of the prisoner's crimes, the person can be forgiven.
This is the gospel message. Our God has been merciful
to us; we must be merciful to others.

Let us keep this key Christian word ever before us—
*forgiveness.*

> But before all this, they will lay hands on you and perse-
> cute you. They will deliver you to synagogues and pris-
> ons, and you will be brought before kings and
> governors, and all on account of my name (Luke 21:12,
> NIV).

Jesus instructed and informed His disciples about
some of the signs and events leading to the end time.
Not only will there be wars and rumors of wars, pesti-

lence and famine, but the disciples will be persecuted
by the religious authorities, and will be punished by the
synagogue rulers, and by the Romans (or civil) authorities, the kings, and governors.

In the ancient world, the accused and the convicted
would be placed in prison as a formal punishment,
often after a severe beating.

Jesus said that this will happen to His disciples for His
name's sake. They are not to be alarmed or awestricken
when these things shall came to past.

It is frightening and alarming how religious persec-
tion is on the upswing in America. In the daily newspa-
pers, there are accounts of persons being tried in court
because of their religious convictions. Whether to have
prayers in the schools, the use or nonuse of medical
assistance, the right or wrongness to have a nativity
scene on public display, theories of evolution versus the
truth of creation—these are just a few.

It would take many pages to describe the religious
persecution that is going on in countries that do not
have democratic rule or freedom of expression.

Can you imagine being sent to prison for Jesus' sake?
We customarily do not think of persons going to prison,
or being in prison, because of their testimony and witness for Jesus Christ. But our Lord said it would happen,
and it has and is.

Christians in prison must understand that they still
have a witness to bear for their Lord and Savior. They
must not think for one minute that their environment
excuses them from the expression and exemplifying the
good news of Jesus Christ.

Jesus instructs us further in this passage that one need
not premeditate as to what or how one will speak when
the time comes. He will give it to them as it is needed.

Our task as persons seeking to minister to the prisoners must be to instruct and inform them by the sure word of our Lord that He is with them and they must show that they are with Him.

> It was about this time that King Herod arrested some who belonged to the church, intending to persecute them. He had James, the brother of John put to death with the sword. When he saw that this pleased the Jews, he proceeded to seize Peter also. . . . After arresting him, he put him in prison, handing him over to be guarded by four squads of four soldiers each. Herod intended to bring him out for public trial after the Passover. So Peter was kept in prison, but the church was earnestly praying to God for him (Acts 12:1-5, NIV).

The incidents of James being put to death and Peter imprisoned are in keeping with Jesus' warning to them that it would happen.

Herod Agrippa I wanted to win the approval of his constituents. One of the surest ways to do this was to do what they wanted. In this case, the execution of James, the leader of Jerusalem church, certainly was a move in that direction. The Pharisees and the Sadducees would give Herod their support because James and his comrades were certainly upsetting the religious and political climate.

When Herod saw that the killing of James pleased the Jews, he sought to do the same to Peter. He postponed Peter's execution because it was the Feast of Passover, and Herod did not want to do anything that would offend the Jews.

While Peter was in prison awaiting what most certainly would be his execution, the church went into prayer. The Bible states that they prayed earnestly on Peter's behalf.

The serenity of Peter was shown in that even though

the execution would be in the morning, he was asleep between four Roman soldiers. What peace! What assurance! What faith!

An angel was sent to release Peter from his chains and set him free from the prison compound. Peter went to the church in the home of Mary the mother of John Mark as they, to their rejoicing, welcomed and received him. The power of prayer in the providential care of God had prevailed.

The biblical principle for us in developing a ministry strategy is to maintain intercessory prayer for those who are in prison. There are many persons who are reluctant to physically visit a jail or prison, but all can visit by way of prayer. Prison prayer goups can formed where the names and needs of prisoners can be lifted before the throne of grace. God does hear prayer and He does answer.

Prayer must never be used as a substitute for not acting, but prayer is a supplement to our efforts as we seek to bring God's will to fulfillment.

The church prayed for Peter while he was in prison, even while he was on death row. God answered and an angel was sent to release him.

Let the words of Samuel, to his people, be our words to those in prison, "As for me, far be it from me that I should sin against the Lord by failing to pray for you" (1 Sam. 12:23, NIV).

"When we got to Rome, Paul was allowed to live by himself, with a soldier to guard him" (Acts 28:16, NIV). The apostle Paul was a prisoner for Jesus Christ. Throughout Paul's missionary endeavors, he had been beaten, threatened, his apostleship questioned, his character and integrity insulted, and his motives disputed.

In this verse, Paul was in Rome under house arrest.

He had gotten there by making an appeal based upon his Roman citizenship. From this Roman imprisonment, Paul, under the direction of the Holy Spirit, wrote what has been called the Prison Epistles—Ephesians, Philippians, and Colossians.

Throughout his writings, Paul never referred to himself as a prisoner of Rome, but always a prisoner of Jesus Christ. He saw his chains as bonds which bound him in faithful loyalty to his Lord Jesus Christ. A quick glance at Ephesians 3:1 and 2 Timothy 1:8 will bear this out.

It is interesting, if you read the latter part of Acts 28, to see that even though confined, Paul still continued to preach and teach the Word. Many heard him and believed and many heard and did not believe. His commission was to all the world and to all creatures. Prison, chains, house arrest, or restricted physical movement would not hinder Paul from fulfilling his task.

How many times have we sincerely sought to do the Master's work but because of opposition or persecution, we detoured, never to come back to the original course? Paul had that inward determination that nothing would separate him from the love of God that was in Christ Jesus.

As we go to minister to the prison-bound, we will need this same kind of determination. Only the burning zeal that will not be quenched will suffice.

Because obstacles and opposition will be present, we must make doubly sure we are adequately dressed. The helmet of salvation, the breastplate of righteousness, the belt of truth buckled around our waist, our feet fitted with the readiness that comes from the gospel of peace, the shield of faith with which we can extinguish all the flaming arrows of the evil one, and the sword of the Spirit, which is the Word of God. And pray in the Spirit on all occasions with all kinds of prayers and requests. Then we will be thoroughly equipped for every good work.

> For Christ died for the sins once for all, the righteous for the unrighteous, to bring you to God. He was put to death in the body but made alive by the Spirit, through whom also he went and preached to the spirits in prison (1 Pet. 3:18-19, NIV).

This passage has been labeled as "difficult" to interpret from an exegetical standpoint. This author does not wish to engage in a battle of hermeneutics.

The significant meaning for those of us who will be engaged in prison ministries is to affirm with rejoicing that Christ has died—paid the price for our sins—to bring the unrighteous into a redemptive relationship with God, our Father.

When Christ was triumphant on the cross, He conquered powers and principalities, the fallen angels, and the whole host of demonic beings which had rebelled against God. Christ proclaimed that to those spirits (fallen angels) in prison that He had conquered them—that He is Lord and King.

There are many persons we will encounter in jails and prisons who are guilty of their charges. The good news we take to them is that Christ died for their sins, the righteous for the unrighteous, to bring them to God.

Sins of the past, present, and future have been liquidated through the sacrificial price Jesus paid on Calvary's cross.

To those who believe they are demon possessed or controlled by evil, or those who have personality disorders, in the strong name of Jesus Christ, they can be released and redeemed.

Do not be afraid of what you are about to suffer. I tell
you, the devil will put some of you in prison to test you,
and you will suffer persecution for ten days. Be faithful,
even to the point of death, and I will give you the crown
of life (Rev. 2:10, NIV).

This final "prison passage" comes from the revelation
of our Lord and Savior, Jesus Christ. He spoke to the
church at Smyrna to take hold and remain firm in the
face of persecution and opposition ahead.

Their period of testing would only be ten days—temporary compared to the eternal joy that awaits them.
They are commanded to be faithful even to the point
of death, having the assurance that they will receive a
crown of life.

As we go to feed the sheep who are in prison, we
need to hear our Lord's words anew and afresh, that we
will suffer persecution for His name's sake, it will only
last for "ten days." Be faithful, He says, in your seeking
to minister, be faithful in your prayers, be faithful in
your compassionate concern, be faithful in your sacrificial service, "and I will give you a crown of life."

I hear Jesus asking Peter, "Do you love Me?" I hear
Peter answering, "Yes, Lord, You know that I do."
"[Then] feed My sheep."

I hear Jesus asking you, "Do you love Me?" I hear you
answering—"What?"

### Guidelines for Future Prison Ministries

1. Establish a contact and relationship with the local
   jailer and find out what chaplain services are available. If there is a staff chaplain, find out how you
   and other Christian brothers and sisters can assist
   in providing a ministry. If there is no chaplaincy

program, go through the proper channels in seeing that a Christian ministry is organized.

2. Inform the church body of their responsibility in the area of ministering to the prisoners in Jesus' name. Teach what the Bible states concerning principles that can be applied to a prison ministry.
3. Have prayer groups pray that persons made be brought under conviction to participate in the prison ministry.
4. Make contact with the state or federal prisons in your area; or if these are some distance away, you can still minister by finding out the Christian ministry programs that already exist and how you can assist them.
5. Contact parole officers as to how you can minister to persons in their custody, and ask for advice as to the best way the church community can be involved.
6. Make a special effort to find out about the detention center or facilities for juveniles. What programs are offered; what follow-up is maintained?
7. Read as much material as possible concerning other churches' prison ministries. Seek out social workers and court-appointed counselors who may give advice as to how you can give assistance in a prison ministry.
8. Dedicate yourself to going in Jesus' name to minister, realizing that as you seek to do His work, He will give you the power and His presence to sustain you.

# Notes

Chapter Two

1. Henri Daniel-Rops, *Daily Life in the Time of Jesus,* trans. by Patrick O'Brien (New York: Hawthorne Books, 1962), n.p.n.

2. Fred H. Wright, *Manners and Customs of Bible Lands*(Chicago: Moody Press, 1953), p. 76.

Chapter Three

1. Christopher J. H. Wright, *An Eye for an Eye: The Place of Old Testament Ethics Today* (n.p., n.d.), n.p.n.

Chapter Four

1. E. P. Barrows, *Sacred Geography and Antiquities*(New York: American Tract Society, 1875), pp. 396-397.

2. Ibid., p. 192.

3. Edmond Stapfer, *Palestine in the Time of Christ,* trans. by Annie H. Holmden (New York: A. C. Armstrong and Son, 1885), p. 191.

4. Ibid., p. 192.

5. Anis Charles Haddad, *Palestine Speaks* (Anderson, Ind.: The Warner Press, 1936), pp. 105-106.

6. Ibid., pp. 103-104.

7. Stapfer, pp. 192-193.

8. Ibid., pp. 198-199.

9. Rev. James M. Freeman, *Handbook of Bible Manners and Customs* (New York: Nelson and Phillips, 1874) pp. 345, 442.

Chapter Five

1. E. C. Rust, *Nature and Man in Biblical Thought*(London: Butterworth Press, 1953), pp. 68-71.

2. George Gordon Dawson, *Healing: Pagan and Christian*(London: Society for Promoting Christian Knowledge, 1935), pp. 20-23.

3. Adolf Harnack, *The Expansion of Christianity in the First Three Centuries,* trans. James Moffatt (New York: G. P. Putnam's Sons, 1904), p. 124.

4. Benjamin S. Baker, *Shepherding the Sheep: Pastoral Care in the Black Tradition* (Nashville: Broadman Press, 1983), p. 116.

# About the Author

Dr. Benjamin S. Baker is pastor of the Main Street Baptist Church, Lexington, Kentucky. He regularly teaches courses in preaching and pastoral ministries at The Southern Baptist Theological Seminary, Louisville.

He teaches and preaches across the country for conventions, clinics, seminars, and revivals. He received the Ph.D. from Southern Seminary.

He has written extensively for pastoral ministries and preaching journals. He speaks regularly on radio and television. His first Broadman book, *Shepherding the Sheep: Pastoral Care in the Black Tradition*, has been highly acclaimed.